AN HOUR'S STROLL ON DARTMOOR

John Hayward

Curlew Publications

First published in 1988 by Curlew Publications
Reprinted with some revision, 1992

Other Books by John Hayward:
    A New Key to Wild Flowers, 1987
    101 Dartmoor Letterboxes, 1988
    Your Dartmoor Century, 1989
    Dartmoor 365, 1991

FRONT COVER: Menhir near Merrivale
BACK COVER: near Haytor Rocks

ISBN 0 9514037 0 2

Typeset by Exe Valley Dataset, Exeter
Printed in Great Britain by BPCC Wheatons Ltd, Exeter

THE MAGIC OF THE MOORLAND

Kipling comes to Dartmoor

Oh, Dartmoor is a country that is full of glorious views,
Of tors, and rocks, and riversides, and stones in avenues,
With ravens o'er the hilltops, and heron by the brook,—
   And the magic of the moorland may be found by those who look.

For where the ling and whortle grow across the windswept moor,
Where skylarks sing, or pipits cheep, or mewing buzzards soar,
Where mighty stones go striding 'cross a landscape grey and bleak,—
   There the magic of the moorland may be found by those who seek.

So lift your head and listen to the wind among the trees,
Or stoop to watch a spider on the bogmoss round your knees.
Learn to use your senses, touch and smell, and ear and eye,—
   For the magic of the moorland can be found by those who try.

There's not a pair of legs so young, nor yet a heart so old
But it may venture out—in Summer heat or Winter cold—
To walk ten paces from the car, then stop and wonder there,—
   For the magic of the moorland is for those who stand and stare.

3

INTRODUCTION

These 'guided walks' are for those who only have an hour or two to spare, but who want to sample as much as possible of Dartmoor's history and nature. You will not have to pack a day's rations, or navigate by compass, or slog across difficult terrain to complete any of the strolls. There may sometimes be wet grass or muddy places to cross, and a rest for a bite and a drink is always a pleasure, so equip yourself accordingly.

When reconnoitring the walks for this book I set out with the object of finding something of interest at least every five minutes during an hour's stroll, and of including plenty of illustrations to help with identification.

In brief, on these walks:

1. You will never be more than a mile from your car.

2. There are no hills along the route that are both long and steep.

3. Although compass directions are sometimes mentioned they are not used for navigation. It is not expected that you will be carrying a compass.

4. An O.S. map is always worth carrying, especially if you like identifying distant tors, but the sketch map at the beginning of each stroll is on a larger scale than any of these, and is all that you will need.

5. You could if you wished get round any of the routes in little more than an hour. But these strolls are designed for those who like to stop and look at things properly, so allow plenty of extra time for doing just that.

Starting places

All the starting points offer easy parking, usually in a proper car park. Many of these have toilet facilities,—and often an icecream van! Occasionally a well used layby is chosen. A look at the STARTING POINT MAP on page 7 will show that most of them lie on the popular routes across the Moor. The numbering goes in a serpentine fashion from West to East.

Weather

These strolls are unashamedly planned for fair weather walking, for there is so much to see. The essence of enjoying Dartmoor is having time to stand and stare. But do be prepared for sudden squalls or mist at any time of the year. One or two of the walks are across open downland, and if the mist is already down then it is not sensible to head out into the unknown.

Place names

Names of many places on Dartmoor are spelt in different ways in different books. This is because some authors prefer to use older or more 'historically correct' spellings. In this book place names are spelt as on the current ordnance maps.

Maps

All the sketch maps are to the same scale, aproximately five inches to a mile. The length of each side of the map is clearly shown.

Routes are marked as in this key:

Road	============
Track	- - - - - - - - -
Suggested walk	....

Verses

The songs and verses were written just for fun, but it is hoped that, armed with a little knowledge of Dartmoor and memories of some well known songs and poems, you will enjoy them.

5

List of Starting Places

see map opposite

THE ROADS OF DARTMOOR

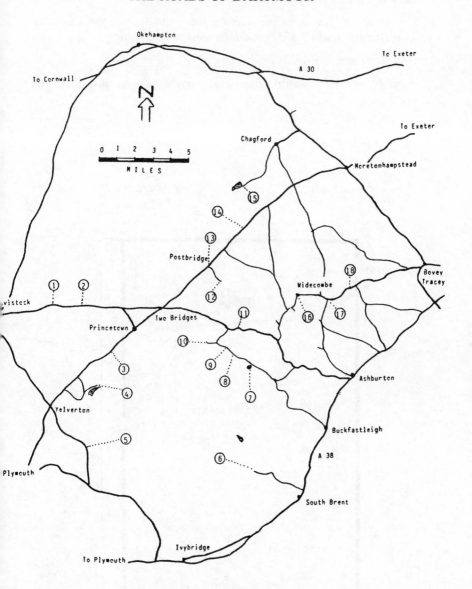

MAP OF STARTING POINTS

Stroll on Barnhill

Easy going on open grassy moorland

Car Park: at the large car park on the south side of the Tavistock—
Two Bridges road (B 3357) one mile west of Merrivale.

Grid Reference: 531751

Items of Interest: Tudor cross, wheelwright's stone, aqueduct, bull's-
eyes.

Great Staple Tor   *Middle Staple Tor*

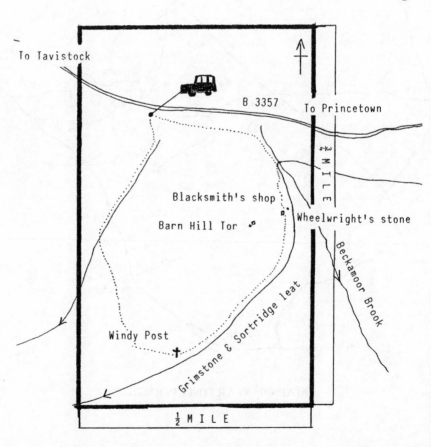

The car park, in open country on the edge of the high moor, affords fine views. To the north, up the hill, is Cox Tor, and to the right the three Staple Tors, of which Great and Middle stand out clearly. In the southeast just to the right of the TV mast is King's Tor. Round to the west in Cornwall the mine chimney on Kit Hill can be seen ten miles away; and to the northwest the tiny church on Brent Tor is about five miles away.

Start the walk by heading east towards the TV mast. Along the very edge of the car park runs a pipe which carries a streamlet down from the gullies on the other side of the road. A few moments later you cross an obvious ditch: this is the dry bed of a leat which once joined the running one to be seen presently. Another minute or two will bring you to the bank of Beckamoor Brook where there are many signs of alluvial tinning. Turn right along the top of the bank and you'll soon see a tiny aqueduct carrying water across the brook.

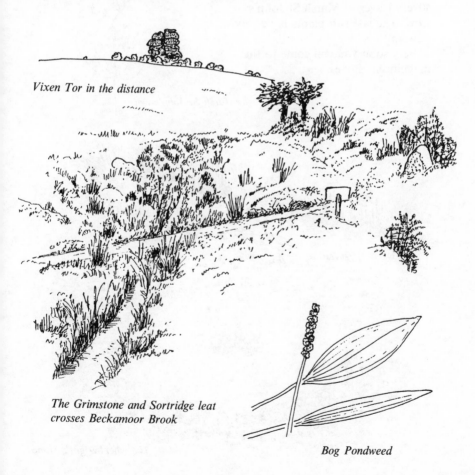

Vixen Tor in the distance

The Grimstone and Sortridge leat crosses Beckamoor Brook

Bog Pondweed

9

Go down to have a look. The leat is a small one and was dug perhaps five hundred years ago to take water to the manors of Grimstone and Sortridge. It comes off the River Walkham about two miles higher up, and along its course several side channels have been taken off to supply water to other farms. This little aqueduct is a delicate one and easily damaged, so please have regard for the notice which says "DRINKING WATER. PLEASE DO NOT OBSTRUCT OR INTERFERE WITH THIS WATER SUPPLY". If you choose your point of view carefully there is a strong impression that the water is flowing uphill. This illusion is not uncommon on the Moor and I often wonder how the men who dug these leats planned such routes that seem to mock the law of gravity.

Now follow the leat for a while. Have a look at the plants growing in it. Bog Pondweed and Spearwort are common, while here and there are the silvery leaves of Marsh St John's-wort. The last two plants have yellow flowers.

Very soon you will come to this magnificent stone.

Marsh St John's-wort

The wheelwright's stone

It measures 5 feet across and is thought to be a wheelwright's stone. It has not been discarded as damaged, like many other relics on the Moor, but was used on this site. Look uphill a few yards: the untidy piles of stones are all that is left of a blacksmith's shop, built here in the 1870's when groups of stonecutters were working on the slopes of the tors on the other side of the road.

The sketch shows an imaginary reconstruction of the smithy.

The circular stone offers an intriguing puzzle to which I have no answer. Why were the three holes in the upper surface drilled at those particular points? Their spacing, as shown on the diagram, supplies only a mystery, not a solution. The figures are not compass bearings, but angles relative to the uppermost hole.

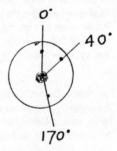

Drilled holes
in the
wheelwright's stone

Now continue along the leatside. To your left across the valley is Vixen Tor. This dark brooding tor loses much impressiveness by not being on a hilltop, because the vertical face is in fact the highest of any on Dartmoor. A grim legend is told of how for many years it was the home of a witch called Vixana. She used to lure travellers to their death in the mire below the tor by conjuring up a mist as they picked their way across the valley. If you really want to experience their plight try crossing the mire on a fine day, and when you get to the squashy part imagine yourself suddenly enveloped in mist. But be warned: crossing the mire in a real mist is not to be recommended.

THE SONG OF LOWAWATHA

by J. H. Shortfellow

Should you ask me, "Whence these stories?"
I should answer, I should tell you,
"From the misty moors of Devon,
From the torrents, woods, and hillsides
Where the Dipper and the Wheatear
Make their home among the boulders."

There was born my Lowawatha;
Spent his childhood, grew to manhood,
Learned to love the tors and rivers.

Once a piskie by the Walkham
Fell into the rushing water.
Lowawatha entered boldly,
Plucked him from the swirling current,
Rescued him from being carried
To the shores of Gitche Gumee,
To the white-waved Big Sea Water.
For this deed of noble valour,
"I will give you," said the piskie,
"Power to see through mist and darkness.
Use it well to travel safely,
Helping others out of danger."

Lowawatha thanked the piskie,
Journeyed on across the moorland
Till he came to Merrivallee
Where he tarried in the hostel.
There he heard the story spoken,
Heard the tale of foul Vixana,
Hideous witch of Vixentoree,
She who watched from Vixen's summit
Waiting for a lonely trav'ler
Coming down from Windiposta
To the mire of Beckamooree.
Conjured mists across the
    pathway,
Cackled as the hapless trav'ler
Stumbled into quaking bogland,
Sank beneath the em'rald
    Sphagnum.

Thither then strode Lowawatha,
Took the path to Samfordspinee,
Took the path he knew would lead him
Through the mire of Beckamooree,
Past the beetling, craggy rock-pile,
Past the home of vile Vixana.

When Vixana saw him striding
Through the Asphodel and Bogmoss
She with magic brought a mist down,
Hid the mire and path across it.

Lowawatha, nothing hindered,
Quickly gained the rocky hillside,
Reached the summit from the hindside.
Saw Vixana peering downward
Waiting for his cries of anguish
From the wat'ry bog beneath them.

"Hi!" said Lowawatha softly,
Waited till she turned towards him,
Hurled her off with mighty effort,
Heard her shriek as down she hurtled,
Plunged beneath the floating Sphagnum
There to bide for ever after.

Vixen Tor

12

Soon Heckwood Tor comes into sight, and then Feather Tor; and in a few minutes a waymark that has possibly been standing where you see it for five hundred years. This seven foot high cross is unusual in two ways: it is still unbroken, and its shaft is octagonal. But the bench mark cut low on one face is sad evidence of 19th century vandalism.

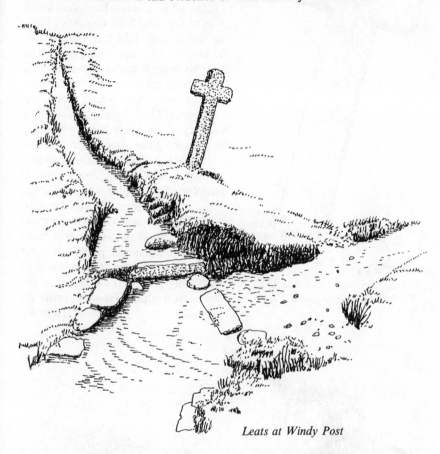

Leats at Windy Post

About 1900 William Crossing, one of Dartmoor's most careful observers, reported that the shaft immediately under the western arm was seven inches off the vertical. By 1987 this had increased to ten inches. There might be a case here for a responsible authority to reset this archaeological treasure before Father Time and Mother Nature combine to wreak inevitable havoc. For this cross, now usually called Windy Post, was almost certainly a waymark on the track from Tavistock to both Chagford and Ashburton. For several hundred years pack horses laden with bales of wool would have come this way on their trans-Dartmoor route. Indeed, just before reaching the cross you saw signs of a track, and

Windy Post or Beckamoor Cross

a clapper across the leat. There is still more to see here, so don't yet hurry on.

The leat here forks into two, the main channel now running off to the right, while a secondary one (which was in fact dug first) continues more or less in a straight line. Notice how the amount of water which is allowed into this branch leat is regulated. It is piped through a hole drilled into the rectangular stone which blocks the channel. These holes are known as "bull's-eyes" or "inch holes". Another notice board gives a reminder that this water is a vital resource. The side branch makes its way down towards Sampford Spiney and supplies farms, cottages, and kennels.

The slab under which the main channel flows shows the drill holes made when it was prised off some nearby boulder. This method of splitting granite is explained in the stroll round Trowlesworthy on page 45.

Bull's-eye or inch hole

14

Now follow the right hand channel. Pew Tor soon comes into view to the left, and about 150 yards from Windy Post is another fork in the leat. Here too is a bull's-eye stone. This one has a bench mark cut into its upper face. If the bull's-eye is not visible put your finger an inch or two below the surface and you will find the inch hole!

Another bull's-eye stone

Sundew

Once again follow the right hand branch and head towards a wall corner. Between the corner and the gate there is a little archway low down in the wall that has been filled in. This would have been a "sheep creep" built to allow sheep and dogs a passage but not cattle. (Drawing on the next page).

Turn uphill along the track towards the next corner, noticing the "grounders" at the base of the wall. What an effort it must have been to move these huge boulders into place. I wonder how many men and crowbars would have been needed; and how far the builders thought it worth moving the stones. I should like to have watched a wall like this being built.

At the next corner keep to the track that goes uphill and in a few minutes the car park will come into sight. When you come to a tiny stream walk beside it. Along its banks grows Sundew. The reddish leaves covered with sticky glands for trapping insects are to be found during much of the year, but the small spikes of creamy flowers on long stalks are more elusive.

A sheep creep

You soon cross once again the bed of the dry leat seen at the beginning of the stroll, and then discover that the streamlet you are walking beside comes out of that iron pipe you also crossed.

Before driving away go to the western end of the car park where a plinth has been set up displaying and labelling the landscape features. There is a name and a date on it . . .

. . . and nearby there is often an ice cream van.

Small Heath

Small Tortoiseshell

Two butterflies you will often come across

16

Stroll near Merrivale

Easy walking on grassy downland

Car Park: on the main Tavistock—Princetown road, B3357, in the car park on the hill just east of Merrivale.

Grid Reference: 553750

Items of Interest: stone rows and circles, a menhir, a kistvaen, an apple crusher, and a 3,000 year old deserted village.

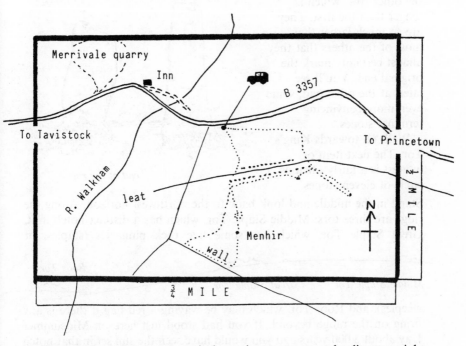

The complex of stone rows, circles, cairns, graves, and solitary upright monoliths to be seen on this walk has intrigued archaeologists for a long time. Many theories as to their purpose have been put forward, and doubtless many more will yet be propounded: every time I visit this site I think of a new one. I also think up five more unanswerable questions.

The easy nature of the walking, the proximity of the site to a main road, and the additional presence of a Bronze Age village and some 19th century relics, makes the area an excellent introduction to Dartmoor's antiquities.

So climb up the bank behind the car park and walk towards the highest part of the rise ahead. In a few moments King's Tor will spring up in front of you. Head towards it.

You very soon pass a small circle of about ten fallen stones, and off to the left a solitary standing one which might better be described as a leaning stone. These are hardly impressive monuments but they all fit in to the many entertaining theories that have been proposed to account for their presence. More of this later.

Just ahead you'll come to the western end of the first of two nearly parallel double stone rows. Look along it. The stones, about 160 of them, are unusually small for a Dartmoor row. Cross the leat—a 19th century one—and bear half right towards a pair of much larger stones.

These form the ends of the other row, which is longer than the first. They are so much larger than most of the others that they almost certainly mark the original end. You'll see later, at the other end, some even more convincing terminal stones.

Walk on towards King's Tor. The next item of interest is a fairly obvious circle of eleven stones.

end of the row

Stand in the middle and look back to the northwest horizon. Along the ridge are three tors: Middle Staple Tor, which has a distinct notch in it, Great Staple Tor, which has some fine rock pinnacles (staples, or

Middle Staple Tor   *Great Staple Tor*   *Roos Tor*

steeples), and Roos Tor, which may be waving a red flag if there is any firing on the range beyond. If you had stood just here on Midsummer Day about 3,000 years ago you would have seen the sun set in that notch on Middle Staple Tor. The slight variation in the Earth's movements since then means that today you would have to move a few yards away to see the same phenomenon. But this seems a good reason to believe that the siting of this circle is not fortuitous. And what about sunrise? No such luck. On that day it first appears above the bare northeast horizon about half way between Little Mis Tor and the TV mast.

But the mid-day sun is well marked. It will be right above the tall menhir which is due south of you . . . and you don't have to wait until midsummer—any day will do. Have a look at this stone. It stands over ten feet tall and is one of the Moor's finest. The word "menhir'" means the same as "longstone", a name by which many of these tall monoliths are known.

I should like to have watched the Bronze Age toilers setting up a stone such as this. It must extend several feet into the ground. The little moat which surrounds it has been worn by cattle making use of a convenient scratching post. About ten yards to the east is a much smaller menhir, now lying flat on the turf; and about 180 yards beyond that is another one, still standing. Were they once in line?

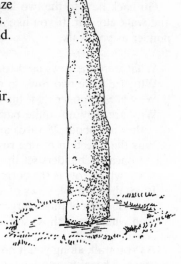

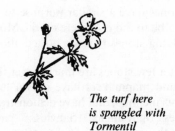

The turf here is spangled with Tormentil

The Longstone, or Menhir

Now for an "optional extra". Go down the slope, straight towards the wall. Built into it is a "sheep creep", a passage arranged so that sheep, but not cattle, could pass through to a different pasture. At the moment it is blocked by a boulder. Then turn right and walk along the wall. There are a number of hefty "grounders" that must have needed much effort to lever into position. You will pass a small cement post that says DOE AM 1972, and can amuse yourself deciding what that might mean. I find it ugly, incongruous and unnecessary.

Not far beyond you will see, used as a grounder, a discarded millstone. Perhaps it is a broken one.

a sheep-creep

millstone in a wall

19

Go back now to the two large stones at the end of the southern row, and walk along it. If you like asking yourself questions here are some to ponder as you walk.

What were the rows used for?

Why are there two rows so close?

Why is one longer than the other?

Why are they not quite parallel? (At the east end of the shorter row they are about 25 yards apart, and at the west end about 33 yards.)

Was the direction of one row miscalculated, and rather than shift the stones the builders set up a second row?

If so, which row is the correct one? And why is it correct?

If so, these double rows of small stones have a similar purpose to the single rows of much larger ones to be found elsewhere on the Moor?

And what about those solitary standing stones that are dotted about?

As you walk along you'll notice that a few stones are much larger than average. Theorists, mathematicians, and mapmakers have drawn lines, on paper, between these and the various menhirs, and have demonstrated equilateral triangles, isosceles triangles, right-angled triangles, a parallelogram, and lots of lines that follow the movements of the moon.

Some of the small stones are surprisingly close, but these have doubtless tilted and settled with time. The overflowing leat has made the soil soft, but remember it was not dug until the stones had been in place for some 3,000 years.

A short way along a row of four stones goes off to the right at an odd angle. There are signs that it was once about 40 yards long. But what has it got to do with the other rows? If you are really keen and have a passion for moon watching they say you can use these few stones to predict all sorts of things. Almost exactly half way along you come to a small stone circle with a pit in the middle. This too is a feature unique among Dartmoor's rows. It was probably a burial pit, but no firm explanation of its siting can be offered.

Just off to the right a great slab is to be seen. Have a look at it. This is one of the Moor's largest kistvaens. These are graves in the form of a sunken box covered with a huge flat stone. Almost all are too small to have contained a body. The dead were cremated and

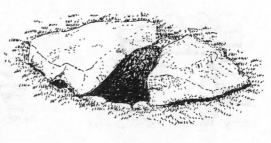

Kistvaen

20

the ashes put in a pot inside. Often there is a ring of small upright stones round the grave, marking the circumference of a mound of earth that would have been heaped up over everything. They are missing here. The cover stone has clearly been despoiled. Round about 1860 a local farmer decided that a slice from it would make a fine gatepost. The drilled holes along the split edges are still visible. They could possibly be used to identify the post—but first you have to find it!

Continue to the end of the row. Both of the double rows terminate with a large central blocking stone. Why at this end and not at the other? Look back along the row and you'll see that

Looking westward along the southern row

Blocking stone

it is not quite straight. But once it may well have been. Slow soil movement could account for the irregularity.

Now look half right, towards the yellow farmhouse, and pick out a tall standing stone not far away. Visit it to confirm that it is of a very different nature from the others. It was set up, it is believed, in 1699 to mark a route across the moor from Tavistock to Ashburton. The T and A face those respective towns. You may be able to spot about three more of these waymarks between here and the farmhouse.

There is another small menhir to be seen from here, about 100 yards away towards the outcrop which is half way down the skyline sloping west from King's Tor. A tree across the valley stands exactly behind it. It looks more impressive close to, and may possibly have formed a geometrical pattern with some of the others.

Waymark, 1699

Running along the slope just below King's Tor is a pale line. This is the dismantled railway that used to connect Princetown with Plymouth. It also served the quarries, some of whose enormous spoil heaps are clearly to be seen.

Now go back to the blocking stones at the end of the two rows, and then on towards Great Mis Tor—the large tor to the right of the three already noted. It too may be flying a red flag. After a hundred yards or so you will find yourself in the middle of a Bronze Age village. The hut circles vary considerably in size. Some show clearly their double wall construction: smooth faced boulders on the inside, more knobbly ones on the outside, and the gap between filled with soil and rubble. In some the position of the entrance can be surmised: look for one or two upright stones on the side facing south to southwest. The roof construction is more problematical. One or several posts were probably used (Trees were more widespread on the moor then) and a thatch of heather and rushes.

An imaginary Bronze Age village

Nobody knows whether this settlement was thriving at the same time as the rows, circles and menhirs were in use. There are faint signs of ancient banks (reaves) nearby, suggesting tribal boundaries, but these prehistoric activities may well have extended across a thousand years, and no one item can be confidently declared contemporary with another.

Well before reaching the road turn downhill and look out for a different sort of curiosity. This mighty mill-stone, dating from the 19th century, is thought to have been intended as an apple crusher. A hole would have been cut through the centre and it would have

19th century apple crusher

been set vertically in a circular
trough, to be turned by a horse
or ox—the first stage in cider
making. There is no obvious
reason why it was abandoned
before completion, but perhaps
someone was glad not to have to
lift it on to a cart.

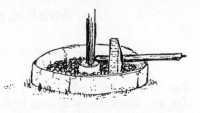

Crushing apples

The car park is now only a minute or so away.

If the time of day is right a visit to the "Dartmoor Inn" down by the
river might make a pleasant finale to the walk. On the way there notice
another T/A waymark by the roadside on your left.

*Waymark
facing Tavistock*

As you cross the new bridge over the
Walkham look across to the older one on the
right. In between is the site of the ford, which
would have been there before even the earlier
bridge was built.

Merrivale Bridge and the Dartmoor Inn

23

Stroll near Black Tor

A walk across grassy downland and beside a stream

Car Park: On the B3212, 2 miles S.W. of Princetown, between Leeden Tor and Black Tor is a small layby. If you are coming from the west this is just a second or two after Black Tor disappears from sight!

Grid Reference: 570718

Items of Interest: a tor, a logan stone, a double stone row, a waterfall, a rushing leat, an aqueduct, and a wotsit.

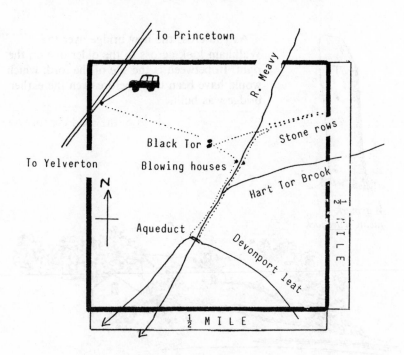

A 1/2-milestone?

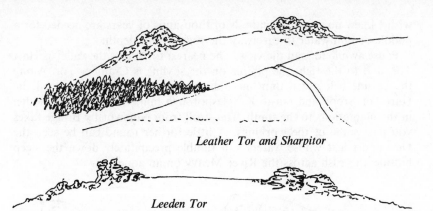

Leather Tor and Sharpitor

Leeden Tor

There are several hard patches by the road here where a car or two may be parked. If you have chosen the one I usually go for then Black Tor will be just out of sight up the slope, but Leather Tor, Sharpitor and Leeden Tor will make a grand skyline from southwest to west. The O.S. map prints MS just here. I think the milestone in question must be the broken stone opposite the layby.

Head east towards the brow of the hill past a large boulder, and then past a cluster of rocks where tare and feather holes show that one or two slabs have been prised off. A hundred yards from the road the tor comes into sight. Go first to the lefthand stack.

The two enormous boulders that rest on the pedestal look as if some giant hand has balanced them there. The smaller one was long renowned as a logan stone, and the map still marks it as such. A logan stone is one that can be rocked—or "logged"—by human effort. But in recent years it has slipped an inch or two and now rests against its larger neighbour. Clamber up to have a look at its upper surface. There is a rock basin there with a large lip, which is probably deepening now that the stone is tilted. I

Logan stone on Black Tor

wish I knew how many hundreds of thousands of years are needed for a puddle of rain water to eat away the rock to this depth.

Pause awhile to scan the view. The nearest tor across the valley is Hart Tor, and to the right the pimple on the skyline is Cramber Tor. Along the hillside below it a thin line indicates an old leat that came off the Hart Tor Brook and ran to Keaglesborough mine, which is now hidden in the plantations to the south. The stroll from Norsworthy Bridge takes you past some of the workings. A little further round can be seen the Devonport leat whose waters still tumble precipitately down the steep hillside and rush across the River Meavy on an aqueduct.

Rock formations at Black Tor

Cross to the other outcrop of the tor. It is more extensive and also higher, and has on its eastern side a remarkable series of stacks and fissures.

Now look again down to the river. Slightly to the left of and below Cramber Tor is a ford, and just above this a double stone row. In the same direction, perhaps a bit to the left, but only 50 yards from here is a small Dartmoor "wotsit". Go and have a close look at it. Back in the 1880's plans were made to dam the valley here and create a reservoir for Plymouth. Several trial holes were drilled in order to investigate the nature of the underlying rock. Although this was found to be

A small Wotsit

satisfactory the local outcry was so great that the project was abandoned in favour of the more difficult site at Burrator. The "wotsit" is a cap fitted over one of the boreholes.

Walk on down to the ford, where there is another wotsit, and cross the Meavy. There are some suitable stepping stones nearby. Take the track up to the stone row.

Hart Tor

This is skylark country   *Double stone row*

This is not one of Dartmoor's spectacular Bronze Age rows—the really big ones are more than half an hour's stroll from any road—but it is a typical double row with a despoiled cairn at its upper end. Again I wonder: was there once a body beneath that cairn, and did its owner choose this burial site? Did he live nearby? Was it a favourite view? Is there any significance in the row's running down to the brook?

Go back to the ford, but stay on this side of the river and walk down-stream. After about a hundred yards you come to a waterfall, and down below a blowing house. For the use of these little places see pages 78–80. There are clear advantages in a site like this. The sudden drop in ground level meant that the leat needed to bring in water, at say head height, would only have to be a short one. You can see where this came in, and also the position of the wheelpit. The wheel actuated both bellows and stamps. The furnace was over in the far corner, and on the floor is a broken mortar stone in which the ore was crushed. The doorway is in unusually fine condition. Go through it and examine it from the outside. On the lintel is engraved XIII. This is thought to be a simple registration number.

27

Blowing house
on the east bank
of the River Meavy

Inside

Outside

Mortar stone

The Soft Rush
is the commonest
of Dartmoor rushes

Black Tor Falls

I always take time off here to sit and watch the waterfall, or picnic, or just muse. Cross the river if you like for a different view, but this walk will bring you back along the other bank to give you another stop at the falls.

Continue downstream on the same side—the river's left bank. Soon the Hart Tor Brook joins the Meavy. It is a pity that the concrete and the railings and the iron pipe so brashly spoil the scene, but there are birds as compensation. I have seen all these in this next short stretch.

Cuckoo

Wheatear

Grey Wagtail

Cross by the concrete spillway and keep to the left bank. Ahead of you is an aqueduct known as the "Iron Bridge". The piers of granite are the original ones built in 1792. Only the wooden duct across it has been replaced.

The "Iron Bridge"

Devonport leat rushes down Raddick Hill

Climb up to watch the water rushing down towards you. It has come a good ten miles from the East Dart to get here, but nowhere along its course does it tumble down with such abandon and joy.

This is the Devonport Leat which will soon empty itself into Burrator Reservoir. If you look at the duct across this structure of wood and granite you will see where the name "Iron Bridge" comes from.

29

Cross the bridge and go as far as the outlet of the iron pipe. Take another look back—on this side the leat bed has been stepped—and then follow the pipe back up valley. On some of the joints some lettering can be made out. This reads PCWW HOLWELL 1915.

Don't cross the stream again, but take a path along a bank back to the waterfall. You are once again in Black Tor Hole. Time for another rest or meditation, or even a nap if the weather is warm. It would be hard to find a more delightful spot within 500 yards of a main road where you have only wagtails, pipits, cuckoos, and with luck a dipper, for company.

The ruinous walls here are those of another blowing house. In the masonry grows Wall Pennywort. This is quite a different plant from the much commoner Marsh Pennywort which you will find nearer the water, but the leaves are similar and unlike those of any other Devon plant.

Marsh Pennywort

Wall Pennywort

A two minute scramble up the steep slope will show Black Tor just above you. Take any route you fancy.

From Black Tor head straight for Leeden Tor, and in a few moments your car will be right ahead.

Dipper

30

Stroll from Norsworthy Bridge

The entire route is along a firm track

Car Park: NORSWORTHY BRIDGE is at the eastern end of Burrator reservoir. Take the road round the reservoir and park between the two bridges at the N.E. corner.

Grid Reference: 568694

Items of Interest: a forest walk, a vanished farmhouse, a blowing house, a historic track.

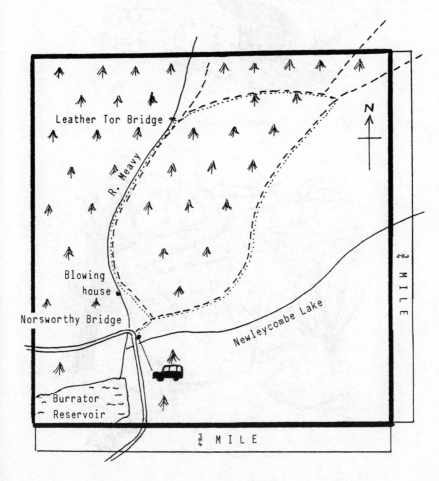

This is a popular starting place for walks in several directions: not often will your car be the only one here, or at the other parking place a hundred yards along. If you are between the two bridges then the larger one, which spans the River Meavy, is Norsworthy Bridge. The smaller stream is Newleycombe Lake (A lake on Dartmoor is always a running stream, never a still pool).

The various paths—along the river, through the woods, up on to the open down, or just to the nearby grassy slope all look attractive. This is a short walk so there will be time to explore them all later.

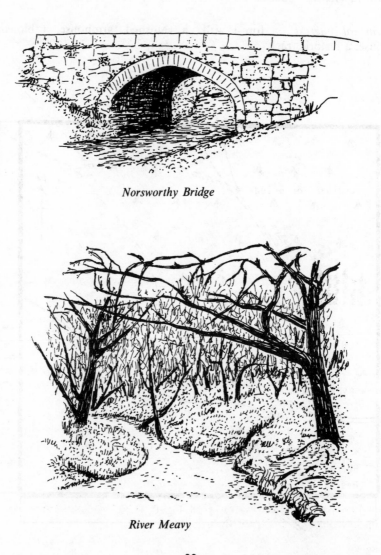

Norsworthy Bridge

River Meavy

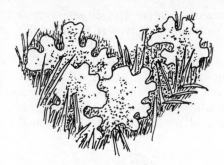

Dog Lichen

Celandines

Start off up the track beside the wall that comes down to the carpark side of the bridge. In Spring Celandines and Violets spangle the banks and Blackthorn trees behind the wall bear a mass of blossom. Look out also, in several grassy patches near here, for the curious olive/grey Dog Lichen.

The greensward on your right is the site of the former Norsworthy farmhouse, which was demolished when Burrator dam was constructed about the turn of the century. It was feared that farming operations would pollute the water draining into the reservoir. Some of the farm fields are on the slope under the conifers.

Norsworthy farmhouse

A short hundred yards up from the bridge the track comes to a junction by an Oak that has blue spots on its trunk. Turn left.

On the right hand side of the track the scanty ruins are probably the remains of farm outbuildings. The plant growing in the wall that has leaves the size and shape of an old penny is Wall Pennywort.

Wall Pennywort

The trees growing here—Ash, Sycamore, Cherry Laurel—are typical signs of former habitation. The wall on the left is part of an earlier house.

After another hundred yards or so you'll see some red-tipped posts on the left. Here are the remains of a blowing house. A search will reveal at least seven mortar stones, of which two have four mortars, showing that the stones were moved only slightly when the first two hollows became too deep for efficient operation. One of these also shows three small

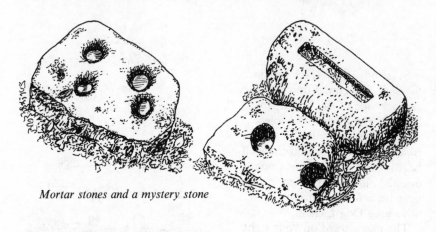

Mortar stones and a mystery stone

grooves which are thought to have been the bearings for one or more axles, perhaps part of the bellows mechanism. The stone with a long slot cut into it is not a mould stone: its purpose is not known. The blocked up wheelpit is on the upstream side of the house. For more information about blowing houses see pages 78–80.

Among the Beeches here is a nearly dead Oak in whose bark some Polypody ferns have taken root. The highest of them must be 30 feet above ground.

In this damp, sheltered atmosphere ferns and mosses flourish, covering bark, soil, and rock.

Continue up the track.

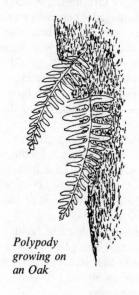

Polypody growing on an Oak

Douglas Fir

Sitka Spruce

European
Larch

Japanese
Larch

The large conifers on the righthand side are Douglas Firs. Their cones—there are many on the ground—are unmistakable with their 3-pronged seed wings projecting from the scales. Cones of Sitka Spruce are also to be found here. These trees are the ones with stiff bluish needles.

On the left of the track in dampish places are patches of Golden Saxifrage. The greenish yellow flowers are out in very early Spring, even before the pale purple or white Milkmaids which also grow here.

In five minutes you will be at Leather Tor Bridge, a large clapper bridge with massive parapets. It was built in 1833 and may possibly have replaced an earlier one. There was certainly a ford and stepping stones here, some of which are still in the river a little way downstream, for some centuries, for it was here that the Monks' Path from the abbey at Buckfast to those at Tavistock and Buckland

Golden Saxifrage

Milkmaids

Leather Tor Bridge

crossed the Meavy. This part of the route is also known as the Abbots' Way. The parapet stones have been locked to each other with iron splints.

Continue along the same bank of the river, and after about fifty

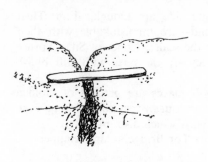

Parapet splint

Pixy Cup lichens

yards take the fork that goes uphill. This is a stretch of the old monastic route mentioned above. Here there are Sitka on the left and Larch on the right. Once again the cones will tell you which is which. Larch is the only conifer commonly planted whose leaves fall off in Winter.

When you reach the S-bend climb the bank on the left to see the long gully running down the hill. This is part of Keaglesborough mine. The leat supplying water for the wheel here is mentioned in the stroll from Black Tor.

Just before reaching the forest edge there is a junction in the track where the Monks' Path goes off to the left. Take the right fork, and so out into the open air. Across the wall and the valley is Down Tor with a several acres of clitter spread across its slope.

Down Tor

Turn right down hill. The massive hill to your left front is Sheepstor. The village of the same name lies behind it. The slopes between Down Tor and the reservoir are patterned with dilapidated walls and neglected fields, indicating a good deal of former farming activity. There are abandoned farms in the valleys on each side of the ridge.

The conifers along the forest edge are now almost all Sitka Spruce.

At a bend in the wall there is a brief glimpse of the reservoir, and then you are back at Norsworthy Farm.

Here is a little fern to be found in the walls round here, Maidenhair Spleenwort.

Maidenhair Spleenwort

Magpie

The crow family are well represented in this area

Rook *Crow* *Jackdaw*

Stroll round Trowlesworthy Warren

An easy walk of under a mile which for extra interest can be extended to about 2 miles.

Car Park: At Cadover Bridge (on the road between Lee Moor and Yelverton) turn east along the "NO EXIT" road for about half a mile until it bends uphill to the right. There take a track to the left and park near the river.

Grid Reference: 564644

Items of Interest: Bronze Age hut circles, a double stone row, rabbit warrening, and a leatside stroll.

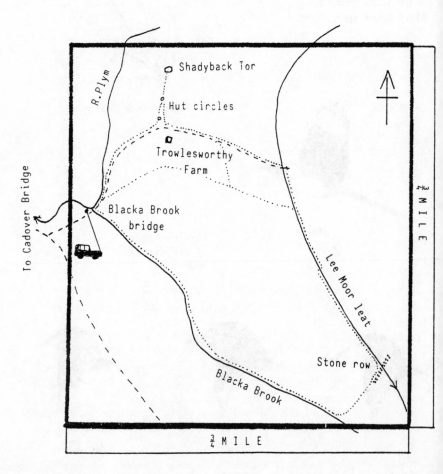

*Blacka Brook
bridge*

Before setting out take a look at
the Plym that meanders down
valley among banks of shingle. A
favourite pastime here is
"improving" the shingle ridges to
form dams across the river. These
are washed away when the river is
in spate and happily rebuilt by the
young in heart when the water
subsides. The little stream coming
down under the bridge is the
Blacka Brook, which has its source
about a mile away.

Trowlesworthy Warren Farm

Take the track across the bridge towards Trowlesworthy Warren
Farm. The National Trust own the buildings and some of the adjacent
walled fields. There has been a farm here since way back in the 1200's,
though the present house is comparatively modern. The two tors on the
skyline to your right are Little and Great Trowlesworthy.

Not far beyond the bridge on the right hand side is a marshy patch
where a number of typical bog plants grow. The yellow Lesser Spearwort
has a long flowering season; its leaves make it easy to identify. Marsh St
John's-wort, also yellow flowered, grows here too, but it needs a sunny
spell to make the flowers open. The leaves of Marsh Pennywort are quite
unmistakable, and a close search in summer may reveal the minute
clusters of creamy flowers which are to be found underneath the leaves.
These three are illustrated on the next page.

As you mount the track you will see in the valley below the scattering
of spoil heaps left by the tin streamers. Many years of toil must have
gone into the raising of these mounds.

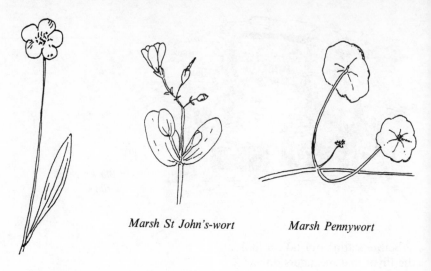

Marsh St John's-wort

Marsh Pennywort

Lesser Spearwort

When the track gets close to the wall a gully goes off to the left. Climb up here for a few yards to see the nearest of a number of Bronze Age hut circles.

Hut circle

There's not much left of this prehistoric home, but the position of the entrance can still be made out. Like many others on the Moor it faces somewhere between south and southwest.

Now continue through the remains of huts and walls, heading just to the right of a bungalow on the opposite side of the valley. Another hut circle you will encounter looks like this. The doorway here too is fairly obvious.

Now...

Perhaps it once looked something like this:

...Then

Keep going in the same direction to the cluster of rocks not far away. This is Shadyback Tor—not named on the O.S. map. Below in the valley the Plym rushes down from the high moor, and on the skyline is the jagged outline of Legis Tor.

Legis Tor

Shadyback Tor

The whole of this walk runs through the lands of Trowlesworthy Warren. The warrens of Dartmoor used to specialize in rearing rabbits. As the nature of the surface was far from ideal for these animals, the warreners would raise "buries", or mounds of earth, to provide soft, warm, dry conditions in which the rabbits could burrow. The O.S. sometimes labels these as "pillow mounds". The ones to be seen presently are 18–20 yards long and about 5 yards wide. Among the pests the warreners had to contend with were stoats and weasels, and on this warren are still to be found the remains of a number of vermin traps. Look out for lines of boulders arranged to form a double V like this:

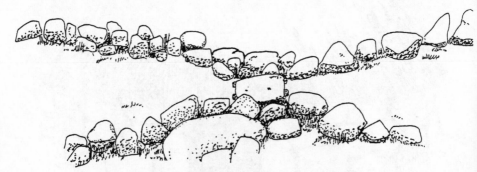

A vermin trap with the coverstone in place

The traps, now all gone, would be at the narrowest part of the funnel. The stoat in passing through the tunnel would trip a wire or lever, and find itself shut in a stone trap.

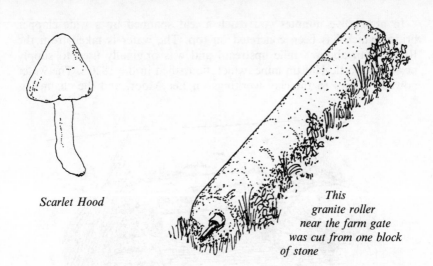

Scarlet Hood

*This
granite roller
near the farm gate
was cut from one block
of stone*

Make your way back to the farm keeping a lookout for these traps on the way. Another interesting find here in late summer is an attractive toadstool called Scarlet Hood. Just before reaching the farm entrance you will pass two of the rabbit buries. Notice the exceptionally high wall which hides most of the farmhouse from this side. A good deal of the farmer's work was done out of doors, and this high walled yard would have been well sheltered from the winds of winter.

At the farm turn left up the track which is now more grassy than stony. Here and there granite chippings have been dumped. Some of these are of an attractive pink colour. This pink granite comes from the Trowlesworthy Tors and used to be much prized. The track takes you up past a ruined wall towards Little Trowlesworthy Tor.

Little Trowlesworthy Tor

43

In about five minutes you reach a leat spanned by a wide clapper bridge which has been concreted on top. The water is taken from the River Plym about a mile upstream and was originally used to supply power to Bottle Hill tin mine, which flourished in the 1820's. The water nowadays goes to the clay workings on Lee Moor, and the channel is

Clapper across Lee Moor leat

known as Lee Moor Leat. As this had to be dug right through the grounds of the warren many little bridges had to be provided to allow both rabbits and warreners (and also sheep and cattle) easy access to both sides. You can see one clapper upstream and several downstream. Cross the bridge and turn right along the bank.

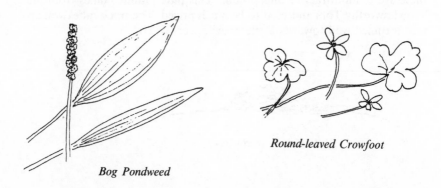

Round-leaved Crowfoot

Bog Pondweed

Two common plants to be found for much of the year in this and many other leats are the white flowered Round-leaved Crowfoot, in bloom from early spring onwards, and the brown leaved Bog Pondweed, whose spikes of tiny flowers appear late in the summer.

44

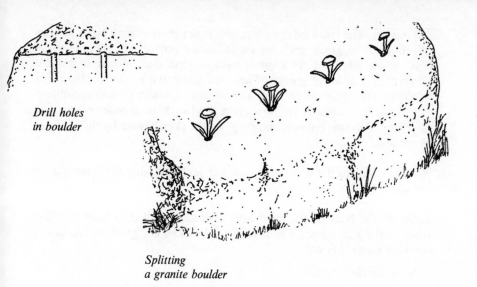

Drill holes
in boulder

Splitting
a granite boulder

In the next half-mile there are fourteen clappers across the leat. Look at the first one you come to. The drill marks where it was split from the parent rock can be seen along one edge. The method used (practised after about 1800) was to drill a row of holes along the line where the rock was to be split by using a hammer and "jumper", a sort of cold chisel. When the holes were a few inches deep an iron "tare" was inserted into each one and wedged with two "feathers" (grooved curved blades of iron). The tares were then driven in harder until the stresses set up caused the rock to split. These lines of half-holes are to be found in rocks all over the Moor where stone cutters have been at work.

Stop again by bridge number 6 and look at the two large boulders which are a few yards uphill. From a distance they look like most other boulders. Indeed they are, but a close examination will show that 99% of their surface is covered with an assortment of lichens, together with a

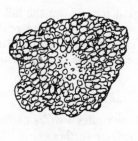

Rock tripe

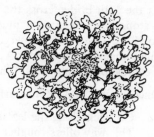

Crottle

few mosses. The speckled grey first seen is not granite at all but a mixture of yellow, olive, green, grey, brown and black lichens. The species are not easy to identify, but as a guide assume that every patch that looks different is a different species. There are about ten species on these two boulders. On the previous page are two that you can probably name.

A number of choices are now open. I'll list them in order of distance (and interest). You are now standing, on the sketch map, by the L of Lee Moor leat.

Route 1   Return the way you came, but perhaps along the other side of the leat.

Route 2   Go back to the third bridge, cross it, and then head downhill towards the wall corner. Even when the bracken is high there is a grassy corridor going this way.

Now another choice:

2a   If the moor surface is very wet make for the upper wall corner and turn right along it until you come to the farm track again. On the way it is worth noticing how the wall was constructed. There is also an abandoned 3-share plough nearby. I wonder just where this was last used?

2b   If the surface is reasonably dry make for the lower wall corner and walk along below the enclosures. At the third corner, where a fence on top of a wall comes down from the right, strike across the grass towards the track you can see—the one along which you drove earlier in the day. There are some wet patches here and there so keep to the shorter turf, well away from the cluster of willows to your right. About 100 yards from the car park turn right along the top of a steep bank towards the farm track.

Route 3   Continue along the leatside. At bridge number 9 look at the drill holes on the clapper, then go about 8 yards uphill to a large boulder which also has drill marks in it. Was the slab across the leat cut from here?

At the 13th bridge cross the leat. Just past here, down the hill, are a few stones belonging to a much despoiled or sunken stone row. Just beyond the 14th (half submerged) bridge is a double stone row running at right angles to your path. At the upper end, above the leat, is a small stone circle once known as "The Pulpit".

Once again a choice of return routes is available:

3a   Go back along the leatside and follow routes 1 or 2a or 2b.
3b   This way offers rougher walking but is no further.
Walk down inside the double stone row. The last time I came this way

I counted 40 stones. I wonder if the builders of these rows could count? And did they too walk up and down between the lines? And if so, why?

Just beyond the lower end of the row, almost by the bank of the tiny Blacka Brook, stands this unmarked bound stone.

Bound stone

Looking down the stone row

Here turn down stream and follow the brook all the way to the car park, a little more than half a mile away. The mounds you cross near the stream were thrown up by tinners in their search for alluvial tin. Two interesting birds that I have disturbed in this little valley are snipe and dipper. Snipe are most likely to be seen flying away from you in zigzag flight. Dippers are unusual in being able to walk underwater even in quite swift currents.

Snipe

Dipper

When you are back by the car a pleasant time can be spent on the shingle of the river bed. There is a greater variety of coloured granite pebbles to be found here than in most Dartmoor riverbeds.

47

Stroll from Shipley Bridge

An ideal stroll for those who like easy going. The whole route lies along a lane closed to traffic.

Car Park: at Shipley Bridge about 3 miles N.W. of South Brent.

Grid Reference: 681629

Items of Interest: River Avon, old clayworks, wild flowers, Avon Dam and Reservoir.

Note: To keep within the limit set by the title of this book the described route stops about half a mile short of the dam.

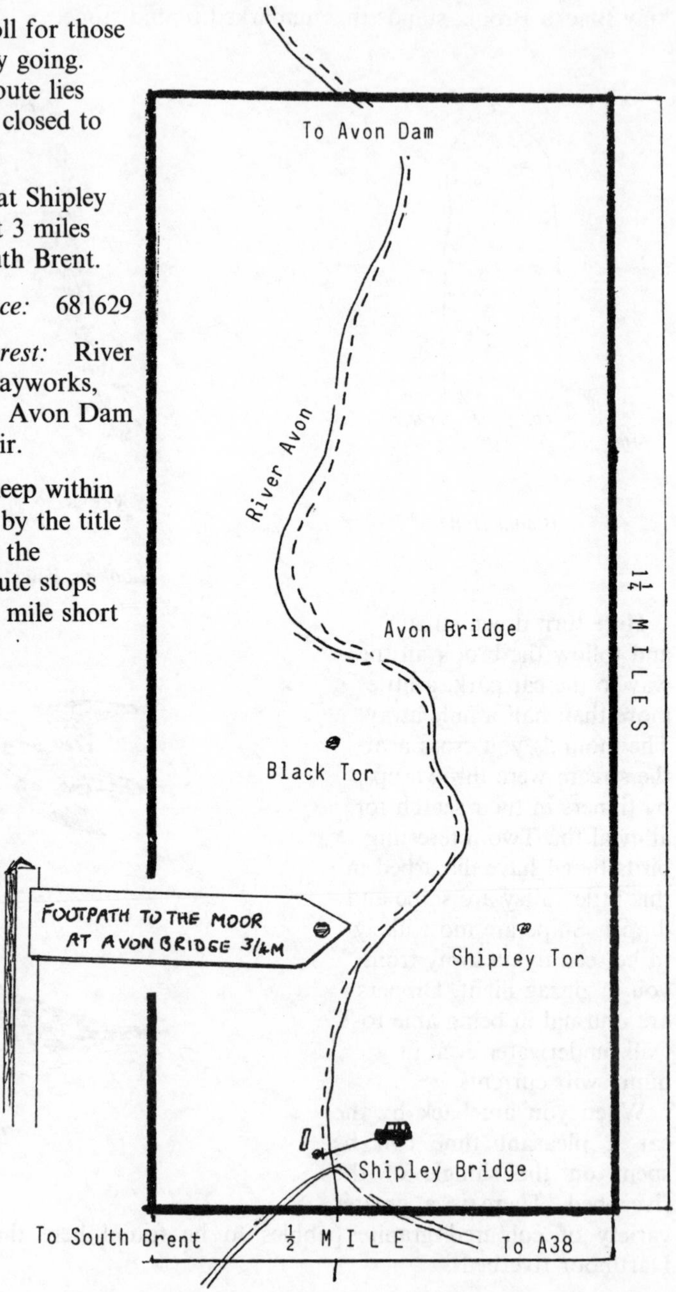

To Avon Dam

River Avon

1¼ MILES

Avon Bridge

Black Tor

FOOTPATH TO THE MOOR AT AVON BRIDGE 3/4M

Shipley Tor

Shipley Bridge

To South Brent   ½ M I L E   To A38

The large car park, and toilets, indicate a well-loved starting place for family picnics, country strolls, and dedicated walkers. After the Avon dam was finished in 1957 the road to it was closed to traffic, so that it now provides a safe, quiet, and very pleasant route for walkers, wheelchairs, and horses.

Old clay works

Here at the car park the most obvious curiosity is the wall at the back with its long, narrow openings. These are the remains of a 19th century china clay processing works. The clay came down from high on the moor in liquid form to settling pits on the slope behind the building, where it drained and dried. If you have time later go up the path that climbs the hill from just below the great wall, and have a look at the pits. There are quite a number of different shapes and sizes. It appears that the clay extracted here was of poor quality, and the industry was short-lived. Before that, about the middle of the last century, this same site was in use as a peat processing works. The peat was brought down in trucks on a wooden railway, for the extraction of naphtha. But that too had lasted for only a few years.

Before leaving the car park take a close look at the streamlet that trickles along just below the bank along the edge of the hard surface. The fine leaved plant that grows in a dark green mat at the waterside is Camomile. Pick a piece of leaf, crush it, and smell it. No wonder our ancestors like to grow it as a lawn. You have only to walk on it on a dry calm day to savour its pleasant aroma. But please don't uproot any to start a Camomile lawn of your own. The soil and climate here suit it well: your garden is likely to be different. In Summer you may find some of its Daisy-like flowers.

HSD—D

49

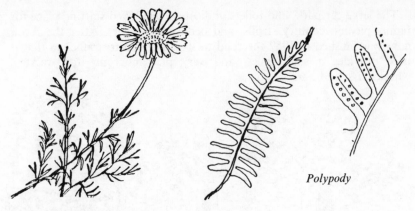

Polypody

Camomile

Now go down to the bridge to start the walk up the Avon. Even down in the dark chasm through which the river is rushing you'll notice the brown colour of the water. This is due to fine particles of suspended peat, most of which has come down from high on the moor. The Oaks along the bank bear a rich covering of epiphytes (plants such as mosses, lichens, and ferns that grow on bark). Look underneath some of the Polypody fronds and you may find the circular spore patches. Another fern here, on the other side of the road, is the Hard Fern. This is unusual in that the reproductive fronds have much narrower leaflets than the normal ones. If you find one of these the spore patches will again be on the underside.

Hard Fern

Soon you come to a small open area at the base of the slope on the left. This is permanently boggy and bears an extremely interesting collection of plants. The next page illustrates some of the flowers to be found here in Summer that have delighted many a botanist.

This habitat is very delicate: trampling will reduce it to mud and destroy many of the plants, so tread carefully, bend down, and use your eyes. All the plants illustrated, except Spearwort, are small to minute.

Just past the "bog garden" a track comes down from the filtration works, and at the junction is a large boulder known as "The

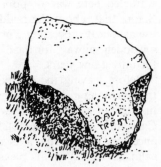

The Hunters' Stone

Marsh St John's-wort
yellow

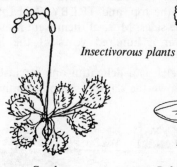

Insectivorous plants

Sundew
white

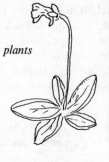

Pale Butterwort
pale violet

SOME PLANTS IN A BOGGY PLACE

Lesser Skullcap
pale purple

Bog Pondweed
greenish

Lesser Spearwort
yellow

Marsh Pennywort
pinkish green

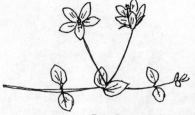

Bog Pimpernel
pink

Hunters Stone". The names inscribed on it all have a connection with local foxhunting—DAVEY, CAREW, PENNANT, CORYTON and LILBURN on the top, and TREBY, TRELAWNEY, BULTEEL and M.H. round the sides. Most of them were Masters of the Hunt and their lives cover over a hundred years of the history of the Dartmoor Foxhounds.

The next stretch is a delightful one for just sitting and watching the water tumble down the slabs of smooth granite.

River Avon

Then comes a pair of gateposts, once the entrance to the grounds of Brent Moor House. Pine and Larch have been planted on the steep hillside and Norway Spruce by the river. Rhododendron and Cherry Laurel grow thickly near the road, while towering above them is a row of five Cedars. Behind the first of these, on a well shaded rocky ledge,

M.M.
MARCH 27th 1865

MY LOVELY LITTLE LILY
THOU WERT GATHERED VERY SOON
IN THE FRESH AND DEWY MORNING
NOT IN THE GLARE OF NOON.
THE SAVIOUR SENT HIS ANGELS
TO BEAR THEE HENCE MY OWN,
AND THEY'LL PLANT THEE IN THAT GARDEN
WHERE DECAY IS NEVER KNOWN.

stands this memorial recording the death at an early age of the daughter of the owner of the house, Francis Meynell.

Soon you come to all that is left of the gardens, outbuildings and then the house itself. There is an apple tree by the road and behind it a wall of concrete blocks. Along the base of this wall grows the small but remarkable New Zealand Willowherb. If it has gone to seed then the length of the pods is quite surprising. A curious place to find an insignificant weed whose home is at the other end of the world.

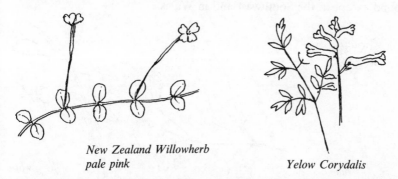

New Zealand Willowherb
pale pink

Yelow Corydalis

Both sides of the river here have been walled. Once upon a time there was a footbridge across to the other side where there were some kitchen gardens. In crevices in the wall another alien plant has established itself, Yellow Corydalis. This one is much more likely to have been an intentional introduction.

The ghost of Brent Moor House

53

Of Brent Moor House itself there is really nothing left worth seeing. So look between the gateposts and imagine something like the sketch on the previous page. The house was demolished because after the dam was completed it remained empty and fell into dangerous disrepair. Even its ghost now has no house to haunt . . . I wonder where it went . . . .

Beyond the grounds Black Tor is to be seen sitting firmly on the hilltop. Nearer at hand, along the grassy bank, look out for the blue flowers of Sheepsbit and Ivy-leaved Bellflower. The latter is hardly ever found except in the Southwest and in Wales.

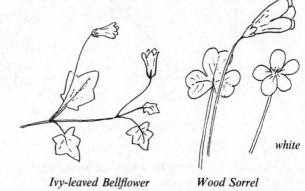

Ivy-leaved Bellflower   *Wood Sorrel*

Sheep's-bit

Lemon-scented Fern

Presently you reach Avon Bridge where a track goes off left and disappears into rough wet ground. Just a few yards along, at the foot of the steep slope is a colony of Lemon-scented Fern. Crush a small piece and smell it to satisfy yourself that you have found the right plant. On the back of many leaflets the neat line of spore patches provides another means of identifying this species.

Keep to the road. There is a small quarry on the right, then a picnic table, and then another quarry.

In five minutes a small building comes into view. This was once used by the Water Authority for measuring and filtering purposes, but it looks a bit neglected now. Beyond here some of the boulders in the river bear a fine crop of a black moss called *Andreaea* in memory of a German apothecary.

The Rhododendrons have now disappeared, but on the far bank of the river is a pair of tumbledown piers which look as if they might have supported a footbridge or a large pipe.

*Cuckoos are to be
seen and heard
in this valley.*

Presently the road swings to the left and Avon Dam comes into sight. It is well worth continuing as far as the dam to appreciate its construction, and then climbing up (the right hand side is easier) to get a view of the expanse of water and moorland beyond. But these strolls are not supposed to take more than about an hour, so the return will be made from here.

Avon Dam

A side excursion on the way back might be the climb up to Black Tor. The best way up is just before you reach the wall enclosing the grounds of Brent Moor House. The view from the top is well worth the effort, and you will be able to find shelter whichever way the wind is blowing.

There are certain to be more wild flowers to find on the way back—Marsh Violet, Common Violet, Wood Sorrel, Round-leaved Crowfoot, Foxgloves, and lots of Maidenhair Spleenwort in the low walls. Then there is an Oak that is doing its best to swallow a hefty boulder.

And finally, from May to October there is a good chance of finding an icecream van in the car park.

Stroll round Venford Reservoir

A sheltered walk, well suited for a winter's day

Car Park: at the west end of Venford dam on the Holne—Hexworthy road.

Grid Reference: 685713

Items of Interest:
   mainly trees.

*Corndon Tor and Sharp Tor
from the car park*

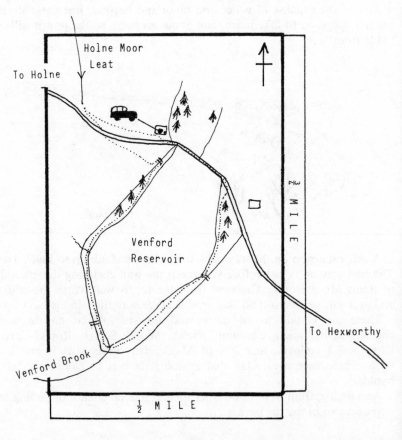

This reservoir started to fill about 1907 when the dam across the valley of the Venford Brook was completed. It was formed originally to supply Paignton though nowadays some of the water goes to the Ashburton, Widecombe, and Brixham areas, and further supplies are piped in here from a small reservoir on the Swincombe, about 5 miles away. Since a good deal of tree planting has been done along the path to be followed, this stroll will take a special interest in them for even in winter it is possible to identify almost every specimen.

Read the information board in the car park. It contains a good deal of background information. The trees round you here are Scots Pine. Although this species is native in Britain these specimens were certainly planted earlier this century.

Before the dam was completed the Holne Moor Leat used to cross the road a short way up the hill, flow in a wide arc round the reservoir, and recross the road on the other slope on its way towards Holne and Buckfast. While the dam was under construction the leat was diverted so that it now disappears underground about 200 yards up the hill to the west, rushes down a pipe, passes under the road across the dam, and reappears on the hillside above the other car park to continue its way along its original channel.

If you have time to spare walk first up the road to study its disappearing trick. About 100 yards uphill you pass a pair of boundary stones. The "P" of "PUDC" is for Paignton. This is one of a number of similar stones which roughly mark the catchment area of the reservoir. The "H" on the other stone stands for "Holne". Not far past these are some Hawthorns. Go to the one on the right of the road to find the tunnel down which the leat disappears. From this spot you can see the old channel running away across the road, and also the line of the underground one which heads down towards the car park. This is the same leat encountered in the strolls from Saddle Bridge and Combestone Tor.

R.D. stands for Richard Dawson, once Lord of the Manor

Disappearing leat

57

Now return to the PUDC stone and follow the shallow gully on the other side of the road down to the trees. At the fence turn left and then pass through the gate into the "Reservoir Walk".

Triple mortar stone

Just inside the fence is a fine mortar stone rescued from drowning before the reservoir was filled. The way these were used is illustrated in the stroll from Saddle Bridge. You will see in the immediate vicinity several saplings that have been added recently to the tree collection. A little way down the path are four large conifers, which in winter will be bare of leaves. These are Larches, the only common deciduous conifer. Two species are widely planted in this country. The simplest way to

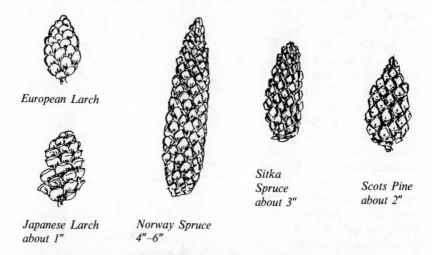

European Larch

Japanese Larch about 1"

Norway Spruce 4"–6"

Sitka Spruce about 3"

Scots Pine about 2"

distinguish them is to find a mature cone and look at the scales. Beyond here most of the evergreens round the water are Spruces. Once again there are two species, both of which you can find here. Spruce leaves grow singly, not in pairs like Scots Pine or in bunches like Larch. The Sitka Spruce has much stiffer more bluish needles and much smaller cones than the Norway Spruce.

See the next page for leaf illustrations.

58

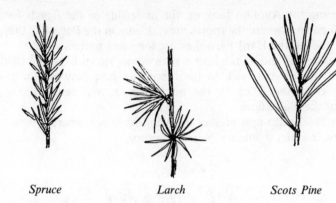

Spruce   *Larch*   *Scots Pine*

Along the water's edge Willow and Rhododendron are frequent. Once established the latter tends to spread and smother other vegetation.

Presently you come to a break in the trees where a streamlet runs down from a mining gully, probably worked during the 16th and 17th centuries.

The last time I came this way I saw at the far end of the water an object that looked just like one of the often published photographs of the Loch Ness monster.

As I approached it turned into a Heron and flew away.

On the bank beneath the Spruce near here can be found at almost any season several different ferns. Here are two that are not difficult to identify.

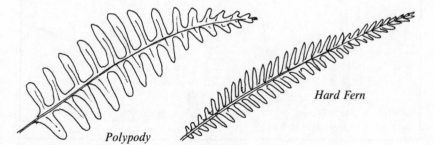

Hard Fern

Polypody

In Summer or Autumn look on the underside of the fronds for the brownish patches where the spores are hidden. On the Polypody they are circular, and on the Hard Fern they are long and narrow.

Just before the end of the lake a path comes down from the right. If you want a short cut back to the car go up here between the young Rowans, cross the fence by the notice board, and return along the outside of the plantation.

A little footbridge now crosses the Venford Brook where it flows into the reservoir under a solitary Norway Spruce.

Venford reservoir and dam

For a short way the path takes you across open ground. Most of the tussocky grass here is Purple Moor-grass, which has a distinctive colour at all seasons. In winter sunshine its pale flaxen tint lightens many an acre of otherwise drab moorland; while ahead, if the sun is right, the leafless Birches are purplish brown.

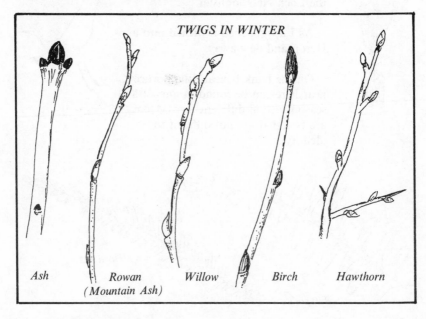

TWIGS IN WINTER

Ash   *Rowan*   *Willow*   *Birch*   *Hawthorn*
          (Mountain Ash)

60

Then comes a plantation of Norway Spruce.

Just before reaching a stile over the
boundary fence there are some fine
specimens of a pale yellow-green lichen
on the Rowan trunks. These are Goat
Lichens. The large healthy patches show
that the air here is still pollution free.

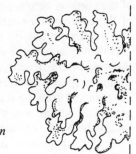

Goat Lichen

Outside the fence another tinners' gully can be seen. But keep going
along the water's edge. When almost back to the road you will find a rain
gauge beside the path and a larch whose growing cones are within reach.
This one is clearly a Japanese Larch.

Venford dam framed by Scots Pine

61

Pass through the gate on to the road by another PUDC stone, and cross the dam. At the near end look over the parapet to the right. Some of the conifers here are Lawson's Cypress. Notice that the topmost shoot of these trees almost always curves over to one side. Only three species of conifer normally do this.

Half way across the dam is a plaque bearing the engineer's name and the date of construction. On the wall opposite is a flat grey lichen of a common species (without an English name) which can be presumed to have started growing soon after the parapet was put in place. The largest patch I could find was about 8 inches in diameter—which means that this specimen has grown outwards 4 inches from its centre in about 80 years. This annual growth of about one twentieth of an inch (about a millimetre) is quite normal for these plants.

A glance down into the deep valley on your right will give some idea of how deep the reservoir might be on the other side. It was clearly an ideal site for building a dam.

On the steep slope at the far end of the dam, on the right, have been planted some Western Hemlocks, one of the other two conifers whose topmost shoot curves to one side. The third species to do this—which is not to be seen round here—is the Deodar.

That makes about 15 different species of trees seen during this short tour. It is likely that in Summer when identification is easier a few more could be expected. Here are some more drawings to help name some of those which are certainly to be found here.

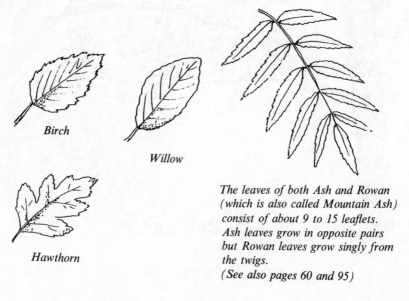

Birch

Willow

Hawthorn

The leaves of both Ash and Rowan (which is also called Mountain Ash) consist of about 9 to 15 leaflets. Ash leaves grow in opposite pairs but Rowan leaves grow singly from the twigs.

(See also pages 60 and 95)

62

LEATS AND BOOTS

Moor advice from Christopher Bobbin

Whenever you jump 'cross a Dartmoor leat
Be ever so careful to watch your feet:
   'Cos you'll learn how it feels
   If you slip on your heels
On mud that is sloping down into the ooze.
If all you are wearing is bare legs and shoes
   Then smother your squeals
   And enjoy how it feels
To sit among pondweed and tadpoles and eels.

But should you be thinking you don't care two hoots
—Because you are wearing green Wellington boots—
And then you slide deep in a watery leat,
You'll suffer much more than just cold clammy feet:
   Your boots will be filled
   With water well chilled;
Your socks and your trousers, your toes and your heels
Will tell you for hours how uncomfy it feels
To wallow in places more suited to seals.

   So whenever you jump 'cross a Dartmoor leat
     Be ever so careful
       to watch your feet.

Stroll from Combestone Tor

A pleasant walk on any fine day

Car Park: at Combestone Tor on the road between Holne and Hexworthy.

Grid Reference: 670718

Items of Interest: Rock basins on a tor, the source of a working leat, a Bronze Age hut circle, a mediaeval cross, a streamside stroll.

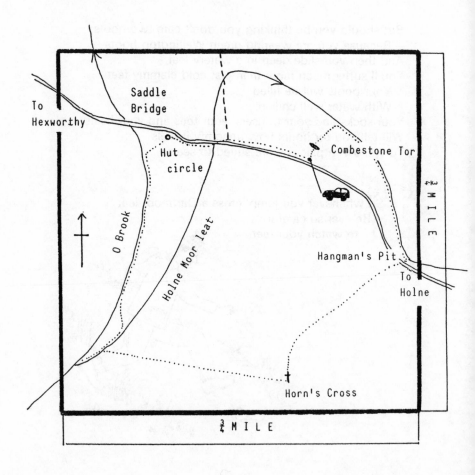

Sharp Tor seen from Combestone Tor

Combestone is probably the nearest tor of any on Dartmoor to a carpark. It is easy to climb, has fine views, and is deservedly popular. Look first through the main stacks across the Dart valley. The knobbly tor beyond is Sharp Tor, and down to the left you can see cars parked at Dartmeet. If you are here when the sun is low you will see that the hillside between is criss-crossed with faint lines. These are some of the Moor's most ancient walls. They date back beyond 1,000 B.C., and are

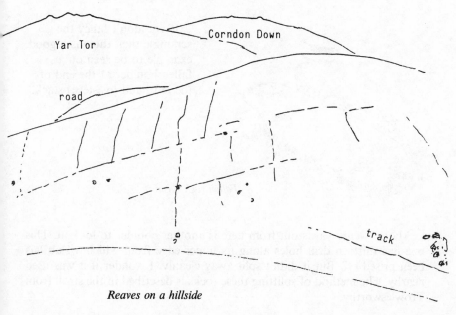

Reaves on a hillside

known as reaves. If either the sun or the bracken is high they may be almost invisible.

Go over to the low right hand stack of granite. On its surface you will notice some pale patches where the rock looks cleanly washed. Indeed it is. These are very slight depressions where rain collects, and slowly, very slowly, aided by wind and frost, dissolves away the granite. In a thousand, or ten thousand, or a hundred thousand years these hollows will deepen into shallow basins. Climb next on to the central stack to see how these "rock basins" look after Father Time has been tending them for uncounted ages.

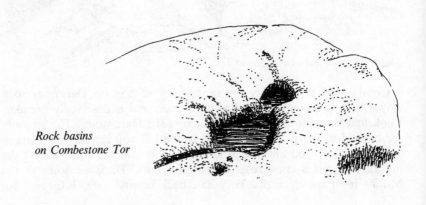

Rock basins
on Combestone Tor

If you don't fancy the scramble then there is a good example to be seen on a fallen boulder at the end of the left hand (western) stack.

Fallen rock basin

About twenty yards out from here is another boulder to look at. This one has thirteen drill holes along its upper edge from which a slab has been prised off. But it didn't split away cleanly. I wonder if it was used nearby. The method of splitting these rocks is described in the stroll from Trowlesworthy.

Now set off downhill just to the right of this dead Hawthorn. You will soon cross a dry channel. This was the Wheal Emma leat which once carried water to a copper mine. It has probably been dry for about 80 years now. What huge boulders had to be moved in its construction. Another moment and you come to a running leat. This one is the Holne Moor leat: it is taken off the O Brook at a point to be visited later in this walk. The leat has been active since the early 1800's when it was dug to supply water to a woollen mill at Buckfastleigh. The mill is now used for other purposes but the water is still needed. Some of it is led off to farms on the way. This leat

is also met in the strolls from Saddle Bridge and Venford Reservoir.

Turn right along the bank. A small clapper spans the water not far along. There is no track here so it is probably mainly for the use of stock.

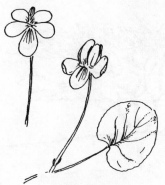

*Marsh Violets
by the waterside*

Clapper across Holne Moor leat

Presently the leat zigzags across a mined gully and curves round the head of a small valley. You can see the line it takes across the hillside, looking for all the world as if it is flowing uphill. Then comes another gully, and a reminder about the water.

Turn up this deep gully. The soil is sandy and after the miners left badgers moved in. There are entrances to the sett on both sides. You should see numerous footprints, and a little searching in the entrances may well produce some black and white hairs.

67

You are now in Hangman's Pit. The story goes that about 1820 a moorman was passing here on his way home from the fair where he had exchanged his horse for another which now appeared much inferior. He was so overcome with chagrin that he hanged himself from a tree in this hollow. Be assured it was not any of the Rowans or Hawthorns that are here now: they are too young.

Badger

If you want a quick return to the car turn right along the road and a few minutes walk will take you there. Otherwise go no more than about 50 yards to where the dry leat crosses the road and there is a tiny quarry. Here strike off at right angles to the road (westward) and head for a boulder on the skyline. In a moment a pair of thorns appears ahead. If the bracken is high a grassy path passes a bit to their left; but they are worth approaching for the pleasing view of Combestone seen between them.

Combestone Tor

A moment later you join a wider grassy track coming across from the tor. Turn left along it towards a tall post. This stands on the line of a reave, like the ones seen earlier across the Dart valley.

Pause awhile to study the view. Up the valley of the O (or Wo as some maps name it) are the pyramidal waste heaps of Hexworthy mine. To the East is the sea. Torquay lies behind the two slender masts. To the northwest runs a fine skyline of ridges and tors.

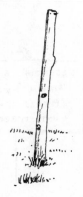

Turn left along the reave for about fifty yards to where a grassy track crosses it, and there bear left towards the cross about 200 yards away. This is Horn's Cross, another ancient waymark. Back in Tudor times it marked the crossing place of two important tracks, one of them being the east-west monk's way from Buckfast to Buckland.

Horn's Cross

A close inspection shows that the cross has had to be repaired. At the beginning of this century only the head and the base were to be found. The broken head was splinted on to a new shaft and remounted in the socket stone. The present column has the stump of an iron spike embedded low down on one side, suggesting a former use as a gatepost. But who knows to what use it was put before that? ... Supporting a mediaeval waymark, perhaps .. ?

This spot is also remembered as a "telling place", that is, a place where a local shepherd would gather his flock to "tell its tale", or count the heads.

If you wish to return direct to the car park from here then go back to the marker post and then on to the tor.

Otherwise follow for a while the monks' old line of march. If the visibility is fair you should be able to see to the right of the spoil heaps a track climbing the hillside. Head in that direction, passing after a 100 yards a small grassy cairn which has been opened up.

Stones of mystery

Presently you come across this group of stones. I have not been able to find any record of its existence, but the two set at right angles look like half a kistvaen (a burial chamber); and the two upright stones were certainly not put there by Mother Nature. In a moment there will be two more boulders off to the right, but perhaps these are natural.

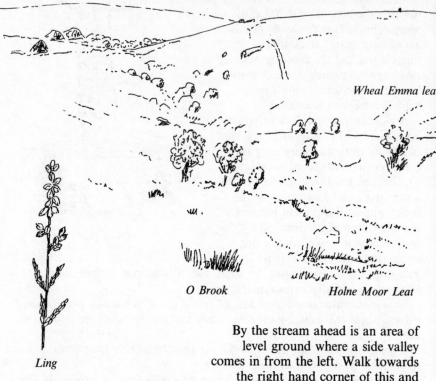

spoil heaps

wheelpit

house ruins
aqueduct

cross

Wheal Emma lea

Ling

O Brook

Holne Moor Leat

Bell
Heather

Cross-leaved
Heath

By the stream ahead is an area of level ground where a side valley comes in from the left. Walk towards the right hand corner of this and pause where the slope gets a little steeper. The scene is filled with reminders of bygone activities. The huge spoil heaps to the left are relics of the days when underground tin mining was carried on a little further upstream. Below these were sheds and dressing floors where operations lasted until about 1920. A bit to the right you may be able to make out a wheelpit, an aqueduct, a track, and the ruins of some cottages. The O Brook sparkles here and there among the willows. On the skyline opposite is another old cross. Slanting gently down the valley side is the line of a leat, and not far below you a glint of

70

water indicates once more the Holne Moor leat, now not far from its source.

The three different heathers shown on the previous page are all to be found on this hillside. Bell Heather is usually the first to flower and Ling the last.

Clapper across
Wheal Emma leat

Walk down to the leat, crossing on the way this clapper over a dry channel. This one is the Wheal Emma leat again. It has come down the hillside opposite, from the right, crossed the O Brook, swung round the valley floor to your left, and is now on its way to the road below Combestone Tor. About three yards below the clapper you will cross the much fainter course of yet another leat!

You are now only about 50 yards from the leat's source, so step across it on to firmer ground and go to the little weir

Holne Moor leat
comes off the O Brook

which directs water from the brook. I can't help wondering if the longest stone in the weir didn't once have some other use.

This is the furthest point of the walk so turn round and follow the leat for a while. If you look ahead you will see the lines of all three leats running along the hillside towards the road. Once again it is difficult to persuade yourself that they are not going uphill.

If you like you can follow the leat all the way back to the road. This makes for easy walking and will avoid part of the climb back up to the tor. But you will miss a stroll beside one of Dartmoor's most delightful streams, and also a substantial Bronze Age hut circle.

So cut down to the river and amble along the banks. There are wet places as well as dry, so don't hurry. This stretch of the O Brook forms part of the boundary of the Forest of Dartmoor, first recorded in 1240. The stroll from Saddle Bridge gives more information about this. The land on the other side of the river belongs to the Duchy of Cornwall.

Birds, flowers, and insects abound here. Once on a February afternoon I found a newt and some frog spawn here, and watched a butterfly (probably a Peacock) dancing past. There are tinners' heaps, some still bare after 500 years. In the stream on some of the larger boulders which are not often submerged grows a black moss called *Andreaea*.

Before reaching Saddle Bridge turn uphill to one of the Moor's largest hut circles. It is to be found just above a large Hawthorn by the road. In the Spring the circle is an impressive one, but in the Autumn it is almost invisible! The doorway faces S.S.E., a slightly different direction from the majority on the Moor.

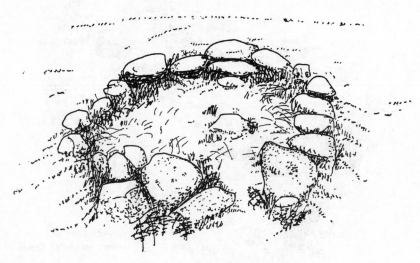

Hut circle

72

Stand back and imagine the hut complete with roof (see page 41), fire, and inhabitants. Add a few more huts on the hillside, more trees by the brook; remove the road and the bracken, . . . and there you have it—a picture 3,000 or so years old.

A short climb up the hill brings you to Combestone Tor. But when you come (yet again!) to the running leat pause for breath to look at the ferns by the waterside on the right of the road. Here grows the

*Frond of
Lemon-scented Fern*

*Pattern of
spore patches*

Lemon-scented Fern. Crush a small piece and smell it. In late Summer the spore patches form a neat border round the edges of the leaflets. No other Dartmoor fern has such a pattern.

The leat passes under the road. So too, in a moment does the dry leat, and a track goes off left down to Dartmeet stepping stones. The tor comes into view just ahead.

Western end of Combestone Tor

BESIDE THE O BROOK

To be sung softly and gently to the tune 'Greensleeves'

Beside the brook the trees hang low,

As dusk comes slowly creeping;

By shallows cool and silent pool

The willows watch are keeping.

Flow, flow, oh restless O,

But bate your song as on you go.

Hush, hush, for night is nigh,

The willows now are sleeping.

Stroll from Saddle Bridge

A varied walk which does not take you more than half a mile from the car.

Car Park: Saddle Bridge is on the road between Holne and Hexworthy. There is a small layby beside the bridge.

Grid Reference: 664719

Items of Interest: Blowing houses and wild flowers.

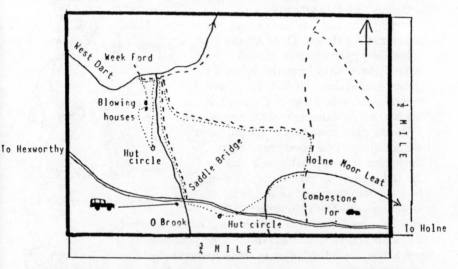

When you have parked have a look around. Beside the bridge is a platform which was once the floor of a small engine house. About three quarters of a mile upstream there used to be a tin mine and in 1905 a generator was installed to supply electricity to the workings. This was driven by a Pelton wheel, which is a type of turbine where each blade on the wheel consists of two cups: these are driven by a jet of water at high pressure.

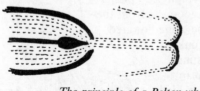 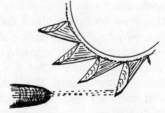

The principle of a Pelton wheel

The water came in a pipe down the hillside from a leat (a dug channel) high above. It was not until the 1920's that the works were finally closed.

Cross the bridge and take the path downstream. You are now walking along the exact boundary of the Forest of Dartmoor. These bounds were fixed when King Henry III ordered a survey party to perambulate his "forest" and to put in writing a list of landmarks along the boundary. Imagine a group of twelve horsemen coming towards you, one day in July 1240, the scribe recording this stretch as "ascendo Okebroke". Nowadays the maps call it O Brook, or sometimes Wo Brook. There are still "okes" along the riverside, though certainly fewer than formerly, before the tinners needed them for fuel. The Forest, now owned by the Duke of Cornwall, is the land on the other side of the stream.

13th Century perambulator

On the right hand side of the path you will see many of the spoil heaps left by the tinners. They probably date back to the 16th century or even earlier. Growing here are both species of Gorse. One flowers roughly from November to July and the other from July to November. Only occasionally do you find both species in flower at the same time in one locality. Is it the Spring or the Autumn Gorse in blossom now?

Look at the stream banks beneath the trees. The left side has been walled up in some places. This is almost certainly connected with tinning operations, more of which will be seen presently. Under the trees stands a solitary gatepost. I wonder where its partner might have been? And where was the wall?

Look closely just here at the trunks of the larger trees. Some are almost entirely covered with epiphytes—plants that grow on bark without taking any goodness from the tree. Mosses, lichens, ferns and even the white flowered Wood Sorrel are to be found on the trunks and larger branches. One of the interesting lichens is the Sausage String: this is a plant that only survives if the air is free of any kind of pollution.

(Drawings on the next page)

Disused gatepost

76

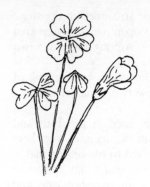

Wood Sorrel

Sausage string lichen

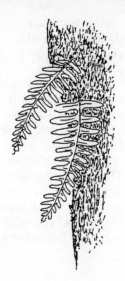

Polypody Fern

At the foot of the O is a modern footbridge. Cross it and walk a short way up the West Dart. Here is open turf and some fine stepping stones. Why not try them for size? How many are there now? There were nineteen last time I came, including the dislodged ones.

Just by the bank grows a clump of Mint. Smell it. It is not a true species, but a hybrid.

Stepping stones across the West Dart at Week Ford

Now turn back a few yards and follow the first streamlet up the slope through the Willows. Soon you will come to an open meadow-like area and 50 yards off to the right a cluster of Oaks. Among these are two blowing houses.

There are ruins of many blowing houses on Dartmoor, but for ease of access and interest it would be hard to beat these two, unusual in being so close to each other.

The principle of these little houses (probably used in the 16th and 17th centuries) is that small lumps of tin ore from the diggings were here crushed to the consistency of sand and then smelted to obtain the metal. The source of power was always water, and to this end a leat had to be dug from a stream uphill. The wheel, always an overshot one and perhaps 9 feet in diameter, would activate both the stamps for crushing the ore and the bellows for keeping the furnace going. It is the bellows that gave these places the name "blowing houses".

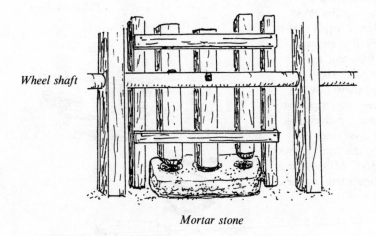

Wheel shaft

Mortar stone

The stamps must have been something like this

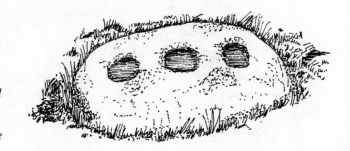

A worn and discarded mortar stone by the upper blowing house

THEN...AND...NOW

Examine first the upper building. It is just possible to make out the line of the leat coming down the hill. The wheel pit is a deep one, and possibly accommodated a larger than average wheel.

The stamps, somewhere inside the house have disappeared (being made largely of wood), but there are half a dozen well used mortar stones scattered about. These would be discarded when the hollows became too deep for efficient working. The furnace was probably in the alcove in the upper wall, and the bellows beside it. The fuel was charcoal and a firing of about 12 hours would be needed to reduce the tin to a liquid which would first be run out into a float (of granite) and then ladled into a mould.

Now step outside and go back some yards from the wheel pit until you have this view. Some of the larger stones have been labelled.

NOW...

Now with plenty of imagination we can turn the clock back 3 or 4 hundred years, and picture it something like this:

...THEN

The lower blowing house

Go down now into the lower house, identify the mould stone, and consider whether you could lift the ingot that would come from it. It would weigh something like 190 pounds—which is thirteen and a half stones. The ingots from the mines in this area would have been taken to the Stannary town of Ashburton, where they were reweighed, stamped, taxed, sometimes resmelted for further refining, and finally sold.

Also in this house are six mortar stones. One of them has more than three hollows. When those on the top side were worn it was evidently turned on its side to expose a new face.

Mould stone in the lower blowing house

Beara House

The wheel pit in
this building, known
as Beara House, is not nearly so well preserved—it was on the right,
looking uphill. Perhaps it once looked like the drawing above.

Now get a wider view of the whole complex by walking out into the
open—that is to the right if you are facing up the slope. I find it
fascinating to draw pictures in my imagination. Did the scene once look
like this? But why were two blowing houses needed so close to each
other? Were they both in use at the same time? If so would the flow of
water into the lower one be sufficient? The drop from the upper to the
lower house is very small. Does this really matter? And why was the
wheelpit not built on the same side in both houses? I wonder . . . but I
have no answers.

Beara House and The Mill from the West

More views from my imagination

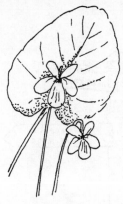

Marsh Violets

If you are not in a hurry it is worth looking at the wild flowers to be found on the open and rather wet slope. Marsh Violets flower early in the year and are easily identified. So is Cottongrass which soon produces its white cottony heads. In summer the yellow spikes of Bog Asphodel are to be seen. Look closely into a single flower if you don't know what to expect. By early autumn the blue flowers of Devil's-bit Scabious show up.

Devil's-bit Scabious

Bog Asphodel

Common Cottongrass

About 200 yards uphill is a fine hut circle, adapted, it was once said, by the "old men" as a cache for their tools at a time when dragons were still to be encountered in this valley .... If the Bracken is high the hut, which is beside a large isolated Hawthorn, will be somewhat hidden, and a visit may be disappointing.

There are more details about hut circles in the stroll round Trowlesworthy.

Return now to the West Dart. You may notice on the way, between the blowing houses and the O Brook, a ten foot length of 24″ diameter pipe. What on earth is it doing here?

Go back across the
bridge and through the
gate by the signpost.
The path along the river
is attractive: let it divert
you if you have time,
and then return nearly
to the gate to take the
path to Holne Moor,
which leads uphill beside
the fence. When you
reach a wall turn left
along it up the steeper
slope. Just past a large
Oak bear half left
towards a 5-barred gate
near a wall junction.

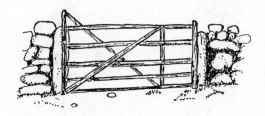

Go through and after
climbing a little further
turn round to look at
the skyline behind you.

You soon pass a deep
gully on your left (a relic
of tinning operations) and
then cross a tiny leat
which supplies water to
Combestone Farm—out

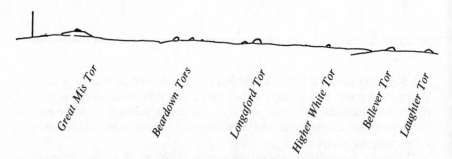

of sight down to the left. Almost immediately you reach a track coming
up from both the farm and the stepping stones at Dartmeet.

Turn right along it over the cattle grid.

In a few moments you cross a larger leat. This is the Holne Moor leat which supplies water to farms and other undertakings near Buckfast-leigh. There is more information about this leat in the stroll from Combestone Tor and also the one round Venford Reservoir. You could continue along the track to the road but the walking will be softer if you follow the leat for a while. As soon as the road comes in sight strike off towards it.

From there Saddle Bridge is in sight, but half way down the hill on the left, just ten yards from the road, is another hut circle. If the Bracken is not high this is worth an inspection.

Continue down to the brook, where a very pleasant picnic place will be found.

Hut circle by the road

85

If you can summon a final burst of energy cross the brook and clamber up the steep slope for a few yards until you are above the platform where the engine house used to be. A search should reveal the pipe down which the water came to drive the Pelton wheel. Take care: the iron pipe is well rusted, has sharp edges, and runs along the bottom of a deep ditch. You can walk up the inside of it because the top surface has quite rusted away. This pipe is only about 16 inches in diameter. Therefore the ten foot length seen lying near the blowing houses cannot have been part of it. Another mystery.

Saddle Bridge

Stroll in the Swincombe valley

Easy walking, much of it along tracks

Car Park: a short way above the "Forest Inn" at Hexworthy (on the Dartmeet to Venford Res. road) take the lane to Sherberton. About 1/4 mile along park on the right just before a gate across the road.

Grid Reference: 651728

Items of Interest: John Bishop's house, Dolly Trebble's house, a blowing house, and some stepping stones.

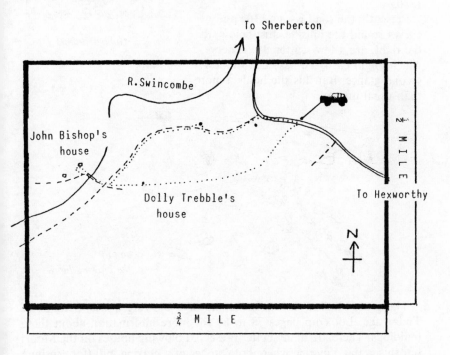

Walk downhill through the gate. Presently look well ahead and you'll see on the hillside across the river about fifty beehives on stilts. These belong to the monks of Buckfast Abbey.

On the left of the lane is a "gert", a deep gully dug by miners, perhaps in the 16th century, to expose a vein of tin ore. Further over, beneath a lone Pine, another gert ends with a tunnel. This handy route was used when the Swincombe reservoir was built to pipe water to the larger reservoir at Venford. Have a look at the tunnel face. The 'P' stands for Paignton. "Gobbett" is the old name of the mineworks here.

Go through the gate labelled 'SWW'. This track leads only to the reservoir, and even if the gate is open cars are not allowed along it. On the right by the Sycamore are the remains of some of the Gobbett mine buildings. They are probably not identifiable: but once in this vicinity there were cottages, workshops, stores, a dressing floor, a wheelpit, and other buildings associated with a 19th century tin mine. The last work done on the site was during the 1880s.

Gobbett tunnel

Presently the road rises a little and curves round the hillside. Just below, to the right, are a few scattered boulders which might easily be passed without a second glance. But this site holds a more than usual interest.

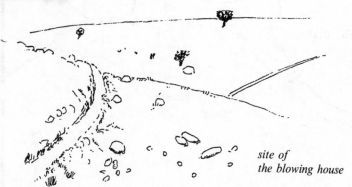

*site of
the blowing house*

The grassy hollow below is the site of a blowing house, perhaps of Tudor age. Look up pages 78 to 80 for more information about these buildings. There are many better preserved blowing houses on the Moor, but this is the only one where both stones of a crazing mill (for crushing tin ore) are still to be found.

Consult the drawings on the next page to identify some of the relics. The lower millstone lies on the sloping bank, and the upper one is a little way below. The four holes in its top surface would have accommodated handles or pegs by means of which the wheel was turned, presumably by a horse or ox.

There are several well worn mortar stones lying about and also a good mould stone, into which the molten tin was poured to set. An ingot taken from this mould would have weighed well over a hundredweight. Some kind of lever would have been slid into the mould, before pouring, in order to lift out the ingot. This stone also has two small sample moulds. They are now very shallow but might have held half a pound or more of tin each.

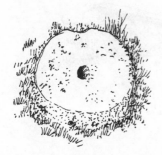

lower stone of crazing mill   *upper stone of crazing mill*

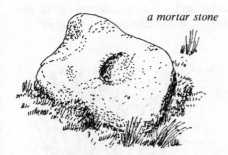

a mortar stone

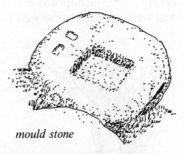

mould stone

More stones like these are illustrated in the Saddle Bridge stroll

Power for the bellows and the heavy stamps was obtained from an overshot waterwheel. The exact site of the wheelpit can no longer be made out but the line of the leat bringing water from the river can be seen if you climb back to the track and continue for only a few yards. But before you come opposite the take-off point of the leat (near a wall end) another leat will have appeared on the left. The track soon crosses this one, which also comes off the Swincombe, but a little higher up. Perhaps it served some of the later workings seen earlier on the walk.

The riverside here makes a pleasant picnic spot. There is not often much water in the river (because of the reservoir further on), but there is sure to be some debris caught in overhanging branches to show how high it can rise when in flood.

From here the ruins of a house are to be seen on the opposite bank. A modern footbridge known as "Fairy Bridge" will take you across the river. There are also some much older stepping stones, still in position and safe to use, and a ford. For here an important moorland route—

the one from Tavistock to Ashburton described in the stroll near Merrivale—crossed the river. Its original track is still clear on both sides of the valley.

Fairy Bridge

Over the bridge walk towards the ruins of the cottage. This is always called John Bishop's house, after one of the tenants in the mid nineteenth century. John Bishop was a turf cutter and a wall builder: many of the local walls, especially the well built ones, bear testimony to his skill.

John Bishop's house

These ruins can be romantic, picturesque, eerie,—according to the season, the weather, and your mood. The porch with its magnificent roof is quite unusual. Inside are two fine fireplaces, but not much else; though the views through the windows are photogenic. Take great care not to dislodge any stone. This little home is slowly and sadly disintegrating.

On leaving the house walk across to the track that comes up from the ford. The other ruins a little further on are of an early twentieth century farmhouse that was dismantled comparatively recently. Turn back to the river, cross it, and walk towards the track that climbs the hill. Take the left hand branch and head towards a pair of gateposts.

As you reach these another pair of stones, even larger, becomes more prominent. Here too are all that remains of a moorland home. The two massive uprights mark the site of the hearth. The building is known as Dolly Trebble's house. Dolly was renowned as a local beauty, and in the early 1800's is said to have attracted the attention of the Prince Regent, later to become George IV.

Gate posts

If that is true then it was probably at a time when she was living about half a mile about Dartmeet in an even more isolated cottage, still known as Dolly's Cot. She may have lived here at Swincombe later when she was working at one of the mines in the O valley, over the hill to the southeast.

Dolly Trebble's hearth

As you leave Dolly's home and go out between the old gateposts speculate on a statement by the knowledgeable writer, William Crossing, that these two stones were removed from a Bronze Age hut nearby, where they once formed a pair of doorposts. Many prehistoric huts and walls have been torn to bits to provide building material for other purposes. But the thought that a pair of 3,000 year old doorposts have been re-used to make a pair of 100 year old gateposts raises all sorts of interesting ideas.

Continue up the slope along the outside of the wall until you come to a corner where a Hawthorn stands. From here you can see your car. Make your way across the slope, keeping the lone Pine to your left.

Dung Bonnets are to be found throughout the summer

91

Stroll at Dartmeet

A very easy level stroll

Car Park: large car park at Dartmeet Bridge on the Ashburton to Two Bridges road.

Grid Reference: 672732

Items of Interest:
stepping stones,
bridges, a sheltered
valley and cream teas.

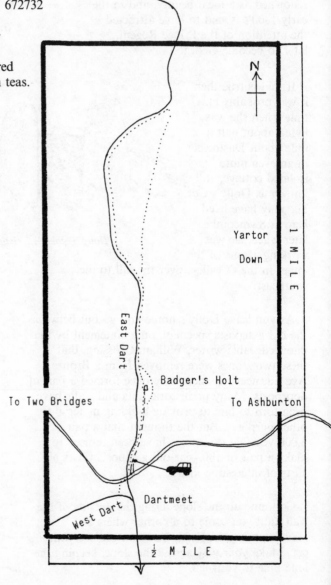

Dartmeet is such a pleasant and easily accessible spot on one of the two main roads that cross the Moor that even those who usually scorn such tourist "honeypots" have been known to make use of its welcome facilities—anything from an icecream to a full meal. Although the restaurant and main shop are closed during the winter the toilets are open all through the year. In fact winter is a good season to come here: the valley is sheltered, the bracken does not cover the hillside, and though the wild flowers may be missing the trees are always on show.

Bridges at Dartmeet

Start by having a look at the two bridges. The situation is similar to that at Postbridge, a few miles higher up the same river, the East Dart. At each site an older (perhaps 15th century) clapper bridge has been superseded by an 18th century one. In this case there is a date, 1792, on the upstream face. From the parapet you can picture the original form of the clapper, a massive construction of five spans. Only two of the imposts (slabs) now remain. The others were washed away in a summer storm in 1826, and although two of them were later replaced they suffered the same fate a second time. Where they disappeared to that time is not known. When the river is in flood the water will rise as high as the road between the parapets, and rolling boulders and uprooted trees may do tremendous damage.

Set off upstream between the river and the car park. If there are more legs than blades of grass along the bank don't worry—it will only be for a few minutes. Notice how rounded the river boulders are, evidence that they have been rolled around for uncounted ages before arriving here . . . and they are not likely to have finished their journey yet. Flowering along the banks in late summer you may see clumps of Golden Rod. This wild species is much smaller than the garden one.

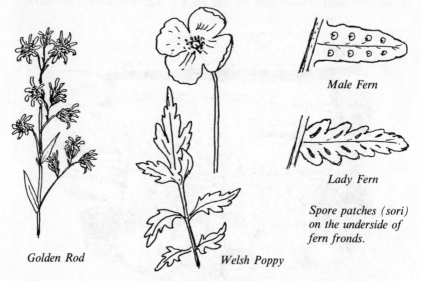

Male Fern

Lady Fern

Spore patches (sori) on the underside of fern fronds.

Golden Rod   *Welsh Poppy*

Beyond the car park take the parth towards the restaurant. Along the wall near the Welsh Poppies are clumps of two large species of fern—Male Fern and Lady Fern. These names have nothing to do with the sex of the plants; but the names are so well established that they have become the "official" English names. The surest way to tell them apart is to look carefully at the underside of a leaflet of a mature frond. Here there will probably be patches of spores. The shape of these little patches will identify the species. See the illustrations. When you know which is which look at the ferns as you go along. Does one species look more ladylike than the other?

There is a small pheasantry on the steep slope, and you may hear a peacock or see one wandering by.

Keep to the left of the restaurant and go through the 6-barred gate, leaving the crowds behind you.

The tree leaves on the next page are all ones you can see on this walk. They include both species of Oak that grow in the National Park. If you examine some Oak leaves you may say that the ones you find look "half way between the two". That is very likely because hybrids are frequent round here!

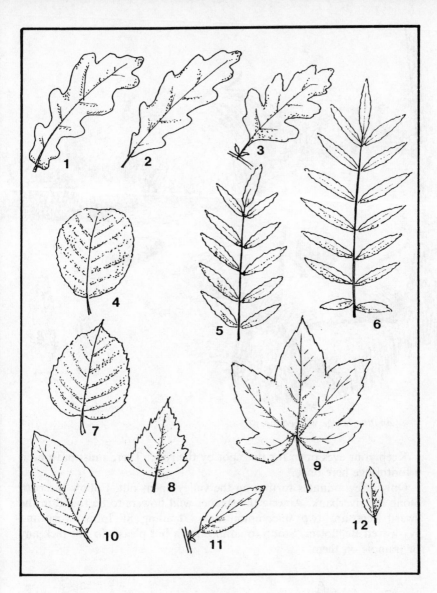

Leaf shapes

1 English Oak	2 Sessile Oak	3 Hawthorn
4 Alder	5 Ash (leaves in pairs)	6 Rowan (leaves in ones)
7 Hazel	8 Silver Birch	9 Sycamore
10 Beech	11 Willow	12 Blackthorn

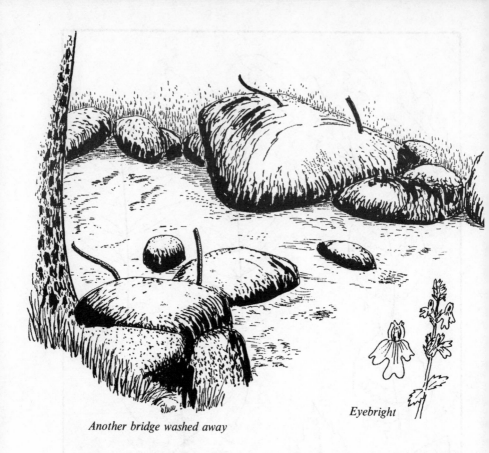

Eyebright

Another bridge washed away

Keep your eyes open for this spot by the river. There must have been a footbridge here once.

Only a few minutes further on the valley opens out. Follow the path along the riverbank. Among the smaller wild flowers to be found in the sward here are two uncommon ones, Trailing St John's-wort and Ivy-leaved Bellflower. Stoop to admire them but please do not pick any or trample on them.

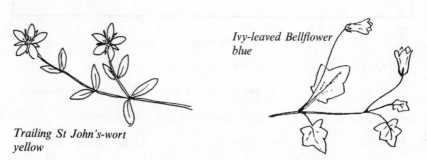

Ivy-leaved Bellflower
blue

Trailing St John's-wort
yellow

The next pause is to look at these stepping stones and ford. They would once have facilitated communication between farms on either side of the river.

Continue as far as the end of the curve in the river, and then return by the path that cuts straight across the bend. If, a little way along, you look back and across the river you can see through the trees, though perhaps only when their branches are bare, the ruins of a house a short way back from the bank. This is Dolly's Cot. For more information about Dolly see the stroll in the Swincombe valley, page 91.

Stepping stones—East Dart

The return journey won't take long. To add variety to it take the path that slants up the hill just before you reach the gate. This will lead you round the back of the pheasantry and down into the car park.

If this feels like an appropriate moment for rest and refreshment . . . then Badger's Holt is a friendly place. The bread, as well as the scones are home made, and the cream teas have a well deserved reputation. This means that it's worth having a good appetite before you order one.

But remember, you haven't yet seen the real "Dart Meet"—that is, the confluence of the East and West Darts. For that is a short way downstream, and in the leafy season is out of sight from the bridge.

To find "Dartmeet" wander on downstream on the same side of the river for a hundred yards or so beyond the bridge. This will bring you to a spot opposite the mouth of the other Dart.

View through the arch

Alternatively, or as a short extra side excursion, cross the bridge and take the signposted footpath on the left. Go through the gate and down the slope to the bank of the West Dart. Here there are more stepping stones.

Stepping stones—West Dart

They are easy to cross if the river is low, and again you can walk down to the confluence not far away.

BATTLE HYMN OF THE PIXIES

To be sung gloriously to one of the rousing tunes of

'Mine eyes have seen the glory',
but NOT 'John Brown's Body'

Mine eyes have seen the glory of the pixies by the road,
They are standing there on Dartmeet Hill with toadstool, frog and
toad,
They are better far than Tupperware and just as good as Spode,
  So tourists, come and buy.
    Glory, glory, grockle-ooya,
    Glory, glory, grockle-ooya,
    Glory, glory, grockle-ooya,
      O, tourists come and buy.

You can see them waiting patiently near New Bridge on
    the Dart,
They are playing in a gateway fit to captivate your heart,
You could liven up your garden with this form
    of modern art,
  So tourists, come and buy.
    Glory, glory, grockle-ooya,
    Glory, glory, grockle-ooya,
    Glory, glory, grockle-ooya,
      O, tourists come and buy.

Down at Wid'combe in the valley they are almost hominoid,
At the cafe and the carpark there are lots of them employed,
They will gaze into your camera with expression anthropoid,
  So tourists, come and buy.
    Glory, glory, grockle-ooya,
    Glory, glory, grockle-ooya,
    Glory, glory, grockle-ooya,
      O, tourists come and buy.

When you go to see the Prison they'll be sitting in a shop,
Midst the teacloths and the ices all entreating you to stop,
You can buy a plastic pixie while you suck a lollipop,
  So tourists, come and buy.
    Glory, glory, grockle-ooya,
    Glory, glory, grockle-ooya,
    Glory, glory, grockle-ooya,
      O, tourists come and buy.

Stroll round Bellever

A very short walk, with optional diversions through the forest and/or up to Bellever Tor

Car Park: Just west of Postbridge take the lane to Bellever. There is a large car park with toilets in the forest about a mile along, before you reach the bridge.

Grid Reference: 656773

Items of Interest: 3 little bridges, a sunny riverside, a shady forest, a chance to climb a fine tor, and some delightful picnic spots.

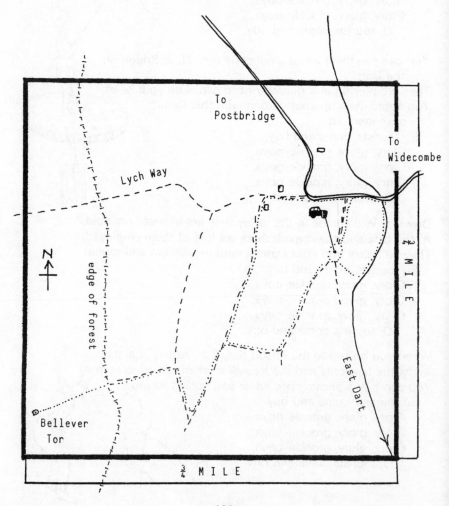

If you park on the right before you reach the end of the track the information board and toilets will be at hand.

The plantations at Bellever are one of the three large forests on the Moor devoted almost entirely to confiers. The first trees were planted in the early 1920's, but many of these have now been felled. Most of the remaining forest was planted during the 1930's and 1940's. The fast growing Sitka Spruce is the most abundant species to be seen on this walk. The page at the end of this stroll will help to sort out most of the important conifers in any of the Dartmoor forests. One tree not included on that page is the Lodgepole Pine. There are just a few of these in the car park. They look very much like the Scots Pine, but a close examination of the needles will show that these are lightly twisted.

Walk back towards the road, noticing the remarkable line of Beech perched on the lefthand wall. The largest of them is likely to be three times as old as the Sitka on the other side.

Turn right and go down to the bridge. If you have already been to Postbridge or Dartmeet, both of which are also on the East Dart, the scene will be familiar,—a ford, a clapper bridge, and a road bridge. Again also some of the imposts, or horizontal slabs, are missing.

Bellever bridge

There were four arches to the clapper bridge, and from the width of the piers there would seem to have been two slabs across each gap. This was once an important river crossing, and the bridge was built to carry substantial traffic. For here is the eastern end of a medieval track called

Through the arches

the Lych Way, which connected the settlements in this valley with Lydford beyond the western edge of Dartmoor. At one time parishioners from these farms were expected to attend church at Lydford, and to carry their dead there for burial. Even after 1260 when they were permitted to go to Widecombe instead, miners, farmers, pedlars, and pack-horses used this route for many centuries. For Lydford, twelve wild miles away, was an important centre: law courts, castle, prison, and market were all there.

From the road look more closely at the two central spans of the clapper bridge. The centre pier has clearly a resting place for the missing

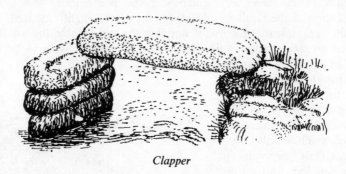

Clapper

slab on its right. But to the left is the widest gap of all. It is possible that stones to bridge this gap were never found.

Cross to the left bank of the river and climb on to the first horizontal slab. From there you can see that both of the stones that would have supported the carriageway have three notches cut into them. Three baulks of wood could have rested there to support a wooden span. Who knows? The missing pieces have long since been washed away. So too have most of the stepping stones.

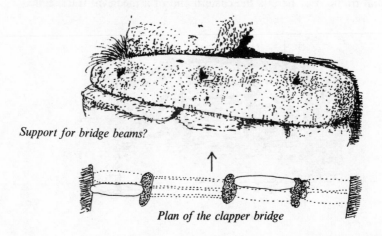

Support for bridge beams?

Plan of the clapper bridge

Stroll downstream along the right (western) bank. The conifers here are still Sitka Spruce. Their "needles" are stiff and sharp and have a bluish tinge to their underside. Beneath the trees in later summer you may find a crop of Blushers, and along the riverside grow Devil's-bit, Golden Rod, and Broom.

Blusher

Devil's-bit Scabious

Golden Rod

Broom flowers

The upper flower has not yet been fertilized. The lower one has been visited by a bee.

This is only a short walk so take it slowly! Here and there at the edge of the forest are some Norway Spruce. Their needles are softer to handle and of a yellower green than the Sitka, and the cones are much larger. (See page 130)

After crossing a streamlet (or two or three) you'll come to a picnic spot that in fine weather is very popular. Linger a while and watch. This is a superb place for children who like messing about in rivers. All they need is a pair of submersible shoes—and some food.

When the grassy banks are crowded you can sit on a boulder in midstream, and when it's drizzly, under the forest canopy . . . and always there is something to watch.

Dipper

103

Turn away from the river by this solitary
gatepost and walk up the little stream. In a
moment you will come to the forest track that
crosses this curious bridge near the car park.

Gatepost
without a gate

Forest bridge

This has been such a short stroll that two ways of extending it are now
suggested. One is to follow the FOREST WALK along the yellow route
(See the dotted circuit on the map), the other is to take the same path but
strike off up to Bellever Tor when half way round. This will give you one
of the finest all-round views to be found in these walks. Allow three
quarters of an hour to walk from the car park to the tor, and plenty of
time to "drink in the view" when you get there.

The damp, sheltered atmosphere of the forest floor provides a habitat
that is rich in mosses, liverworts, and ferns. Here is one of the large and
common mosses, Woodland Hair-moss. It will not have stalked "fruits"
at all seasons, but it should be easy to identify. The Hard Fern is of
course much taller.

Woodland Hair-moss

Hard Fern

Eyebright

104

The way through the forest is well waymarked, and only the last stretch up to the tor is at all steep. Start from the far end of the car park, going off to the right, through a gate and up the slope.

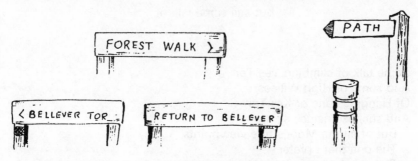

If at this junction you turn left then here is a guide to the view from the top.

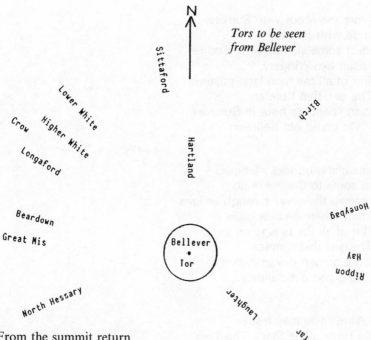

Tors to be seen from Bellever

From the summit return
to the main track, turn downhill
and follow the RETURN TO BELLEVER sign.

When you come to a gate near a farm turn right. This is the Lych Way again, and you are almost back to the road. If you have climbed the tor to admire the view then you have completed the longest stroll in this book.

BELLEVER TOR

The British Grenadiers are not often seen on Dartmoor now,

but still some talk of. . .

Some talk of climbing Yes Tor
And some of High Willees,
Of Hangingstone or Kes Tor,
And suchlike names as these.
    But of all the Moor's fine viewpoints
    The one that I prefer
    On a sunlit day in Springtime
      Is grand old Bellever.

Explore the Moor with Starkey,
Or ride with Hemery,
Collect some stamps with Godfrey,
Or paint like Widgery.
    But of all the moorland pastimes
    The one that I prefer
    Is to spend an hour in Summer
      On grand old Bellever.

Some climb up rocky ledges,
And some to Cranmere go,
Or splash their way through sedges
To find where orchids grow.
    But of all the hills to conquer
    The one that I prefer
    On a golden day in Autumn
      Is grand old Bellever.

In Winter you may rest in
'The Rock', 'The Star', 'The Tors',
Or seek 'The El'phant's Nest' inn
To stay there snug indoors.
    But of all the drinks on offer
    The one that I prefer
    Is a mug of steaming coffee
      On grand old Bellever.

Stroll from Postbridge to Hartland Tor

A riverside walk and an easy tor to climb

Car Park: in the large car park at Postbridge, between Two Bridges and Mortonhampstead. Information Centre and toilets here.

Grid Reference: 648789

Items of Interest: three kinds of bridge, two kinds of feather bed, a riverbank, a tor, and a memorial to a mystery.

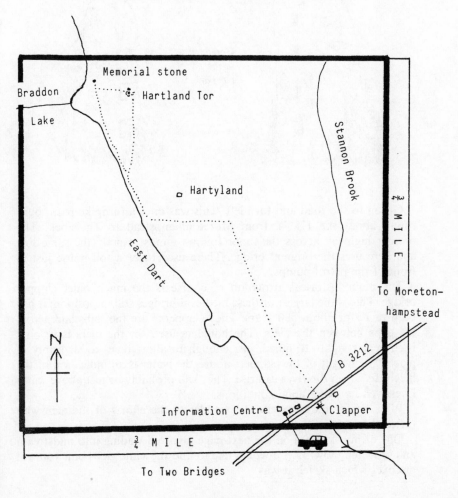

Postbridge is a popular place for a break on a journey across the Moor. It has all you need for an hour or so, and being in open rolling country it does not have that "congested" feeling that can be experienced in the deeper valleys. The information centre is an excellent one, the displayed weather forecast is exceptionally good, the staff are cheerful and helpful, and it is open for about eight months of the year.

Before you even leave the car park have a good look at the pair of gateposts under a Beech to the right of the line of posts near the toilets. The L-shaped slots in the right hand one made the fitting of bars quick and easy, and would have thwarted the efforts of cattle to lift them.

Gateposts in the car park

Go on to the road and turn left. This was once a turnpike road, built round about the 1780's, from Moretonhampstead to Tavistock. The present highway across the moor follows almost exactly the same line and here uses the original bridge. There used to be a toll house just in front of the petrol pumps.

The main historical attraction of course is the much older clapper bridge. This is the largest of these medieval bridges still in position: it has been there for about 500 years. The "clappers" are the slabs laid across the gaps between the piers. The boulders used for the piers have only been very roughly trimmed, just enough to allow them to sit firmly in place. The height of the clappers above the water is an indication of the height to which the river can rise. They will probably be just above water level even in severe flood conditions.

Walk across the clappers and wonder at the efforts of the men who raised them.

One of my sketches on the next page involved wading into midstream and crouching low. If you would like to find the same viewpoint you will discover which sketch it was.

Bridges new and old—turnpike and clapper

A 200 year old bridge seen through a 500 year old one

Now cross to the east side of the road bridge and go through the gate that will lead you upstream. This path will take you through five such gates. Do be meticulous about closing them properly: there will be horses, ponies, sheep, or cattle in the enclosures or on the open moor beyond.

The two flowers on the next page are to be seen in the first few yards inside the gate. The blue Sheep's-bit is often found on banks and walls, but the second flower, which will be growing beside the path, is much more unusual, so do not pick any. The white umbrella-like inflorescence shows that it belongs to the Parsley family, but it is nowhere common enough to have been given a "proper" English name—you'll just have to call it "Corky-fruited Water-dropwort". Yes, that is its "recommended" name! If you want to look it up in a book then try *Oenanthe pimpinelloides*—which is nearly as bad. By the river grows one of its

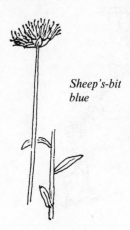

Sheep's-bit
blue

Corky-fruited Water-dropwort
white

much commoner and more robust relatives, Hemlock Water-dropwort. In the drier places round here Fairies' Thimbles, or Foxgloves, are often abundant.

Carefully pick a single foxglove flower. Using two hands squeeze each end of the flower between thumb and forefinger. Then sharply snap your fingers together to burst the flower.

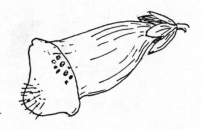

Now you know

why they are called "Poppies".

Almost immediately the path crosses the Stannon Brook by a clapper of five slabs which have been well cemented in place. The saplings which have recently been planted on the right hand side just beyond are appropriately all local species: Rowan, Beech, Birch and Willow, which in years to come will provide shelter to the fields behind.

Then comes another gate, and a blue arrow to follow. At the end of the field turn left along the wall. The house beyond is called "Hartyland", named after Hartland Tor which rises behind it. A picturesque setting, but a lonely place to live. If you fancy it why not try their B & B?

The end of this wall brings you to the riverbank and another gate. Turn upstream. The next gate has a clump of Bamboo beside it, and the last one just beyond lets you out on to the open moor.

Hartyland and Hartland Tor

Head up the grassy Tormentil-spangled slope and climb on to the highest platform of the tor. The little white flower with fleshy leaves that grows on the rock is English Stonecrop.

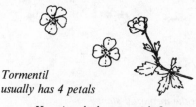

Tormentil
usually has 4 petals

Here is a lucky one with five

English Stonecrop

Looking back from Hartland Tor you can see the road and car park, but the bridges are hidden. Across the valley of the East Dart a stream tumbles down. This is Braddon Lake: a "lake" on Dartmoor is never still. Both to the left and right of this stream ancient pounds can be seen on the hillsides. Once they both contained Bronze Age villages, but only the upper one now has any hut circles left in it. The leat that runs along below this pound was built to take water to the Powder Mills, about two miles away to the southwest.

Looking W.S.W. from Hartland Tor to

Longaford Tor   *Higher White Tor*   *Lower White Tor*

111

Now for the first of the promised "feather beds". It is just below you if you are facing across the valley, is about twenty feet long, and is set flush with the turf. Fine for size, but too hard? Never mind, some softer ones are to be found later.

Make your way down towards the patch of meadow at the foot of Braddon Lake, heading for the right hand corner. When you reach the path in the valley turn upstream.

How to find the memorial stone

Soon you come to a small Willow on the riverbank. Look up valley and slightly to the right to identify two more trees, a Rowan and a Holly. Make for a large boulder to the right of the Holly but much nearer. A part of its surface has been prepared to receive a simple inscription.

Behind this lonely, overgrown, and seldom noticed memorial lies a strange story.

Memorial

William Donaghy was science master at a school in Warrington, Lancs. On 21st November 1913 at lunch time he left school and disappeared. Nothing was heard of him until his body in rain soaked clothing was found near this spot on 21st February 1914. Apart from a guide book, some money, and a groundsheet, he was carrying nothing appropriate to exploring the Moor in winter. Later a bag of personal belongings was recovered from an Exeter railway station. No other clues were ever found to suggest where Donaghy had spent the previous three months, and no explanation of his sudden departure from home where he had relatives, a fiancee, and a job, has ever been provided. Here is a mystery that will certainly remain a mystery.

Return now along the river, cutting across the zigzag opposite Braddon Lake. Keep to the path along the foot of the hill rather than wander across to the river; otherwise you may experience the other sort of featherbed. These are real soft ones of course, but don't be tempted to lie on one! Neither is it likely that your footwear will keep your feet dry if you try to walk across one. Of course if you are fascinated by bog plants you will be prepared for wet knees.

From the first gate you come to your way follows the outward route, but the view ahead is different!

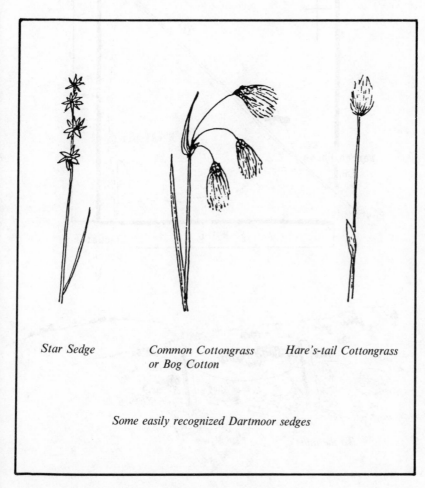

Star Sedge   Common Cottongrass   Hare's-tail Cottongrass
                     or Bog Cotton

Some easily recognized Dartmoor sedges

Stroll near the Warren House Inn

A pleasant walk across dry ground along easily seen tracks

Car Park: about 200 yards northeast of the Warren House Inn on the B3212 between Moretonhampstead and Postbridge.

Grid Reference: 676811

Items of Interest: old tin mine workings, a mediaeval cross, a popular inn, birds.

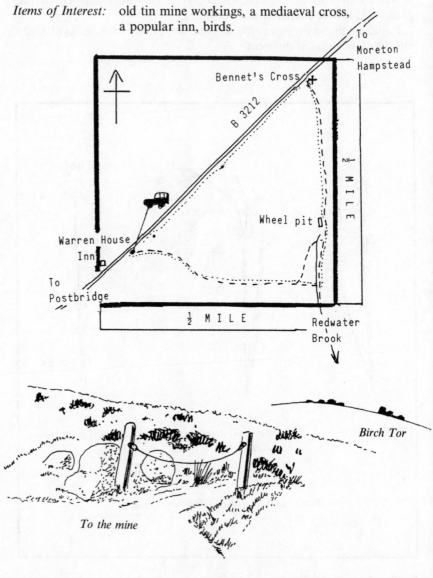

To the mine

Before leaving to explore the mine workings in the valley—or the inn on the hill!—look across the road. Behind the low wall there once stood a bungalow where the mine manager used to live, towards the end of the last century.

After wondering why the line of telegraph poles should end just where it does take the track that goes off from the car park towards Birch Tor (across the valley and to the left). Just beyond the first sharp bend climb on to the bank and look back at the inn. It is easily the highest one in Devon and is said to be the loneliest in all England. Certainly there is not another habitable building in sight. Why then is it here? The answer lies in the valley below, where from the early 1700's until the 1920's active tin mining was going on. But for 500 years before that the "old men" had been working the area: for in a document dated 1240 there is mention of a smelting house on the hill not far from the car park. Within little more than a mile of where you are standing anything up to 150 miners at a time were employed. The great gullies that score the hillsides were bare, and from this spot you could have seen at one time or another four huge waterwheels, chimneys, workshops, engine houses, great stamps for crushing the ore, dressing floors for washing and sorting it, tracks, carts, horses, mules, lines of moving rods connecting the wheels with the pumps in the shafts, and leats of running water to provide power for all these operations. Just a little way beyond the inn, at a site known as Cape Horn, was accommodation for the miners.

Buzzard

Ring Ousel

The bustle and the noise have died, and the buildings have all but disappeared, but a romance remains, softened by the heather and livened by the singing of skylarks, or the occasional mewing of a buzzard or the call of a ring ousel.

Presently some granite slabs across the track show where a leat bringing water to turn the wheels passed beneath you. The channel is now overgrown and "dry", but once water flowed here (from the right). It had been taken off the East Dart 200 feet higher up and about 7 miles away.

Look now to the slopes ahead. There you can pick out a number of small enclosures, well spaced and oddly shaped—tiny fields, carefully walled, whose disposition on the heathered hillside offers yet another mystery. The usual explanation of their origin is as follows.

At Widecombe there once lived a ne'er-do-well called Jan Reynolds. Being a gambler and hard up he had, at an early age, sold his soul to the

Devil. On the afternoon of Sunday 21st October, 1638 Jan was "attending" service in the village church. It seems he was alone in the back pew, taking little notice of the parson, and playing idly with a pack of cards. It was at this moment that the Devil arrived to reclaim Jan's soul. He tethered his horse to a pinnacle on the tower roof. There was a flash of light and a dreadful crash. Jan grabbed his cards, the Devil grabbed Jan, the pinnacle fell into the nave, and the card player was swept away through the skies. Four of the congregation died of injuries. Satan headed north over Birch Tor, where the distraught prisoner on the back of the black horse was seen to drop some of his cards—the four aces. They fluttered to the ground—and those are the four little fields you can see.

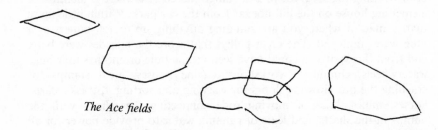

The Ace fields

It takes only a little imaginary redrawing to decide which is which. And the truth? Well there certainly was a great storm on 21st October, 1638 when a pinnacle of Widecombe church did crash to the floor; people were killed or injured; and after all, those fields are plainly there! Explanations that mention folding sheep, grazing stock, keeping rabbits, or growing vegetables may of course satisfy some, but I know which story I prefer.

In a few moments a steeper track cuts directly down to the stream. Pause here to look down valley. About a third of a mile away there is a break in the plantations, where once was another mine called the "Golden Dagger". This one was also active into the 20th century.

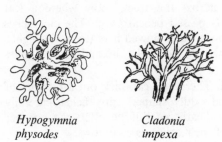

Hypogymnia physodes

Cladonia impexa

Take the short steep track. On each side as you go down you will see, as well as heather two species of greyish lichens. They do not have English names so here are the scientific ones. The first nearly always grows on the soil, the other usually on twigs. 'Impexa' mean 'uncombed', an appropriate name.

116

THE RIME OF THE WIDECOMBE CARD PLAYER

How Coleridge might have told the story of Jan Reynolds

It is perchance Old Nick himself
Who stoppeth foolish Jan.
'By thy cloven feet and horny head
What wantest thou, my man?

'I have no cash to give to you
Or other begging folk.'
'The boot is on the other foot',
Quoth Nick, 'It's you that's broke.

'You've lost your wealth by playing cards,
And now you're into debt.
Perhaps you'd like a hefty loan,
And pay no interest yet?'

The gold was paid, the bargain made
With little rigmarole.
'That's fine', the Devil said, 'One day
I'll come to get your soul.'

The months went by. October came.
At Poundsgate on the hill
Mine hostess took a golden coin
And put it in the till.

'Twas paid her by a handsome guy
Well dressed beyond belief:
That same Old Nick, who played a trick
And changed it to a leaf.

Then off he rode to Widecombe,
And hitched up to the tower.
Inside the village folk had met:
It was the Vespers hour.

O, Jan, have care, the Devil's here,
He's come to claim his due.
But Jan was thinking of his cards
Beside him on the pew.

A flash, a crash, a rending sound,
And Nick was by his side.
'The time has come to keep your pledge.
You'll come with me and ride.'

Jan grabbed his cards. They rose aloft.
A corner stone fell in,
Which killed four people down below—
The price of one man's sin.

Then through the sky, in haste on high
Poor Jan was borne away;
But all unplanned from out his hand
Four acres dropped astray.

Canst see them on the Western slope,
Below the tor named Birch?
Then mark them well, for Jan's in Hell,
Who took his cards to church.

A little way down you come to a stream flowing off to the right. If you walk along its bank for about 30 yards you will see ahead the nearly filled in entrance to an old shaft. This was at the lower end of a number of ore bearing lodes that ran back up the slope. Below, where the stream turns sharp left, are the scanty remains of several buildings.

Continue down the track to the greensward near the brook. Here are a few Willows, more ruined walls, and other odds and ends of bygone activities.

Grey Wagtail

Cross the Redwater Brook by the clapper bridge and turn upstream. Grey Wagtails are often to be seen along here, and even in earliest Spring Round-leaved Water-crowfoot will be flowering in shallow pools. Later

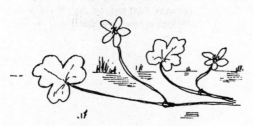

Round-leaved Water-crowfoot

Blinks

in the season Blinks will open its tiny white blossoms in marshy places. The flowers are unusual in that each one has 5 petals but only 2 sepals.

A hundred yards or so along you pass a spring whose waters flow into the Redwater Brook. Nearby a track runs off to the left. If you want to return to the car from here this one will take you back to rejoin the main track down which you came.

To continue to Bennet's Cross take the right fork, ignore the next path to the left, and recross the now diminutive brook a short way past that junction, where a deep gully goes off to the right.

On your left now, almost beside the path is a fine wheelpit with a Hawthorn growing from the far wall. Here was the home of one of the great wheels, 30 or 40 feet in diameter, used to move the rods which in turn worked the pumps. From this wheel these rods extended to two shafts back along the valley and two more up the hill behind the pit. The water came through the little tunnel to the left, so this wheel must have been a breast-shot one.

Leat tunnel

Once it might have been like this

Wheelpit

The pit usually contains water—I don't know how deep—so the exit is evidently blocked. However it is not suitable for swimming!

The path now climbs a slope. Over to the right is another gert (a deep gully dug in the search for ore) with Brich Tor on the hillcrest above. From early March until October Wheatears are likely to be seen among these heaps and gullies. As they fly away their white rump makes identification easy. These birds were once called White-arses, but it is said that our Victorian forbears found such a name too coarse and adapted it to Wheatear!

Wheatear

At a grassy entrance to another gully take the path that climbs up the right hand side and in a minute or so Bennet's Cross will be in sight. Keep to the narrow path across the heath towards the little car park, and then visit the cross. This is one of the most roughly hewn of Dartmoor's ancient crosses, being only crudely—but picturesquely—shaped from a suitable lump of moorstone. An old track between the Benedictine monasteries at Exeter and Tavistock used to be joined near here by another coming over the hill from Chagford, and the stone acted as waymark. Bennet is an old form of Benedict. In addition this stone stands on the parish boundary between North Bovey and Chagford (which runs roughly along the line of the road), and later it was adopted as a boundary marker for Headland Warren (on the south side of Birch Tor). The letters "WB" carved on one face stand for "Warren Bounds". But now there is little evidence round here of rabbit warrening: heather and tinners have taken charge of the landscape.

Bennet's Cross

Turn southwest along the road: you'll find a path through the heather. In a few minutes over to the left is another warren bound stone bearing some fine patches of a pale grey lichen called

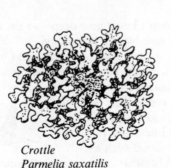

Crottle
Parmelia saxatilis

Warren Bound stone

Crottle. The Ace of Diamonds shows up well from here; and at the roadside is a milestone.

About 100 yards before the car park another warren bound stone stands just to the left.

If the time of day is right it would be a pity to miss the loneliest inn you may ever have the opportunity of visiting. The building was originally on the other side of the road, round about the 1750's, and was called "Newhouse". In the course of time a small rabbit warren was established

Another bound stone

Warren House Inn

nearby, the inn was rebuilt in its present position, in 1845, and was renamed "Warren House". The sign above the door shows the emblem of the Tinners' Rabbits, adapted from a carving on a roof boss in Widecombe church. A mapmaker's bench mark outside is recorded as being 1416' 4" above sea level. You are standing outside the second highest pub in England. The fire in the bar of the original "Newhouse" was of peat, and was never allowed to go out: so when the new hostelry was built the fire was carried across the road and put in the large grate you will find inside. And there it still burns. So on any day of the year you can warm yourself by a fire that has been burning for over 200 years.

Tinners' Rabbits

121

The fire that never goes out

If the afternoon is fine there are some stone benches to sit on with a magnificent view across the valley . . . and don't neglect to examine the lions.

BEDTIME STORY

A new version of an old story about the 'Warren House Inn'

*If you feel like singing then try a tune that is usually reserved
for a well known carol.*

Away on the moorland
As darkness set in
A trav'ler arrived at
The Warren House Inn.
The weather was bitter—
Deep snow on the ground—
His faltering footsteps
Made never a sound.

Mine host bade him welcome,
'Good evening', he said,
And set to preparing
A meal and a bed.
'We've not had a guest here
Ten days in a row,
For no one could get here
Because of the snow.'

Salt mutton for supper
And freshly baked bread
Soon meant that the trav'ler
Was ready for bed.
A cheery 'Goodnight', and
He went up the stairs;
Then knelt by the bedside
To say a few prayers.

He noticed a coffer
With half opened lid,
And sleepily wondered
What in it was hid.
He lifted it higher
And held up the light—
Inside was a body
All glistening white.

The whole of that long night
He ne'er shut an eye;
He dared not relax as
The hours crept by.
But nobody entered
With cudgel or knife,
To claim one more victim,
Or threaten his life.

Next morning at breakfast,
—Salt bacon and toast—
'I hope you slept well', said
His jovial host.
The bleary-eyed trav'ler,
Not sure what to think,
Admitted with candour
He'd not slept a wink.

'I looked in that coffer,
—You know what lies there—
A white, naked body
With glistening hair.
The weather's so bad that
I had to stay here,
But I was determined
To sell my life dear.'

'Forgive me, I pray you',
The landlord replied,
'Twas two weeks ago now
That grandfather died.
The snow lies so deep that
We're cut off from town,
So upstairs we laid him
And salted him down.'

Stroll round Fernworthy Reservoir

All level walking. Three different routes suggested.

Car Park: Car park, toilets, and picnic area all here. The lane to the reservoir can be reached either from Chagford or from the Moretonhampstead to Postbridge road.

Grid Reference: 669838

Items of Interest: This stroll is particularly recommended in the autumn after a dry Summer, when the water will have fallen to expose several hut circles, two bridges, and a track across the valley, all of which spend nine tenths of their time submerged. If the water is high then there is a path all the way round. An excellent kistvaen can be visited at all seasons.

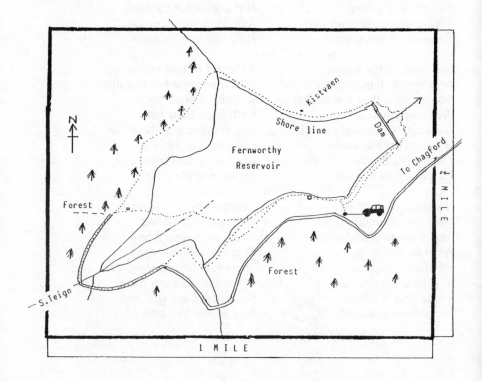

Start off along the shore towards the fishermen's hut. During the fishing season—early May to early October—this will be open. Inside are displayed bird identification charts, maps of the forest walks, and fishing information.

Looking across the reservoir to Thornworthy Tor

Continue along the lakeside. If there are fishermen along the bank please remember that noisy walkers will spoil their pastime. If the water is high you will not be able to walk across the reservoir! In this case skip the next five paragraphs to the one beginning with **.

But at the end of a dry summer the track that crosses the valley to Fernworthy Farm will be exposed and you can walk down this and across the little bridge over the South Teign. In recent years I have sat on the parapet and enjoyed a scene like the one sketched overleaf, in November 1978, September 1982, and October 1987. Where now all is mud and sodden tree stumps there was once good grazing. Oak and Elm grew here and near the farm on the other bank Ash and Sycamore. But the townspeople round Torbay were short of water, the dam was constructed, the farm abandoned, and in 1942 the water began to rise. It normally covers about 76 acres and is up to 60 feet deep.

A number of Bronze Age hut circles—to be seen later on—were submerged, as well as this little bridge and the much smaller and older one about 50 yards upstream. The farm, which may well have been here since Norman times, had to be demolished because its proximity to the water would have created a pollution hazard.

The track across to the farmhouse site among the trees is hard but muddy. Follow the line of boulders and tree stumps marking the causeway. On the way note a "floating island" for resting birds and an observation hut for resting bird-watchers.

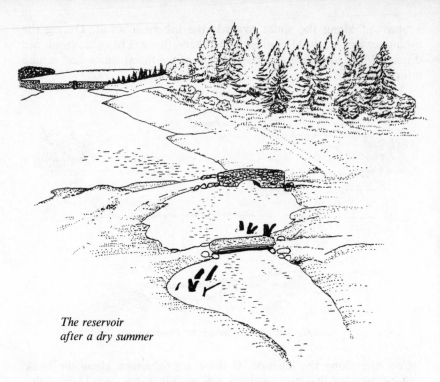

*The reservoir
after a dry summer*

Near the shore, but on the mud, are several colonies of two unusual plants, which are normally underwater. One is Shoreweed which bears tiny four stamened flowers on the end of fragile stems. The other is Quillwort, which has clusters of spores at the leaf bases. A commoner plant that grows here is Marsh Pennywort whose tiny flowers may be hidden among the leaves. (See page 51.)

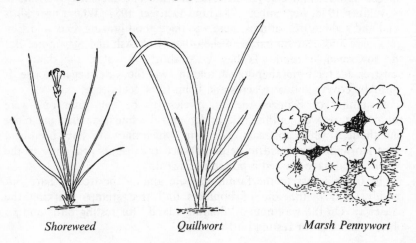

Shoreweed   *Quillwort*   *Marsh Pennywort*

126

Just through the trees are the scanty remains of the farm buildings. Climb up behind them and cross a small open meadow to join the RESERVOIR WALK, which is waymarked with blue-ringed posts, and turn right. Now skip the next five paragraphs and rejoin the text at the paragraph beginning ***.

**On the way along the bank look a little way across the water to see if the Amphibious Bistort is in bloom. Its pink spikes of flowers rise above the surface. As the path turns up the slope you'll pass through a mass of Rosebay Willowherb. In autumn the long pods split open to release thousands of parachuted seeds, rather like Thistledown, but smaller.

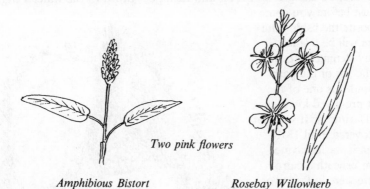

Two pink flowers

Amphibious Bistort   Rosebay Willowherb

A footbridge takes you across Lowton Brook, and then on an open slope are more picnic tables. Follow the path that runs below these towards the hut near the shore. This belongs to the Devon Birdwatching and Preservation Society, but if you are a serious birdwatcher you will be welcome to use it, provided that you leave the door and hatches properly closed. Inside is a logbook recording details of birds seen.

Next take the path that leads up towards a large shed. Go through a gate and turn right along the road. You soon cross Assycombe Brook, which tunnels under the road, and then the South Teign at SANDEMAN BRIDGE. Just beyond is a small stand of Douglas Fir (see page 130). The needles are much softer and less blue than Sitka, and the cones, which are easy to find here, have 3-pronged bracts projecting from behind the scales.

Soon the road ends. The woods here, where there are some fine Beech and Sycamore, are good for fungus hunting. This Stinkhorn was sketched just a few yards away.

Stinkhorn

Cross the stile ahead to a path which crosses an acre of open grass. Below, beneath a line of Beech is an old wall. Behind this are the ruins of Fernworthy Farm, demolished when the reservoir was filled. There is little left, but you may like to go down to see where the submerged track comes up from the other side.

***Continue along the Reservoir Walk. The way ahead, which may be muddy in places after a long wet spell, cuts through a planted area and then skirts the forest edge. The trees here are Sitka. At the end of the plantation, from where Thornworthy Tor is to be seen up to the left, the path crosses Longstone Brook and then goes down to the water's edge.

Just before you come opposite the fishing hut there will be a small many-stemmed Rowan to the left of the path. Behind it is one of the best preserved kistvaens on Dartmoor. It was not discovered until 1878, when it was excavated from beneath a cairn. There were in fact two kistvaens under the same cairn. The other one is now in a museum at Torquay. This grave

Kistvaen on the north shore

with its undamaged sides and carefully propped up coverstone gives an excellent idea of these moorland relics, so many of which have been despoiled. A few flint tools were found in the graves but no signs of any human remains or ashes.

The dam is now not far ahead. The path runs down and up steep banks where Rhododendron have needed little encouragement to establish themselves. It is clear from here that this deep narrow exit from a wide basin makes an ideal site for a dam and reservoir.

If the water is low on the other side keep to

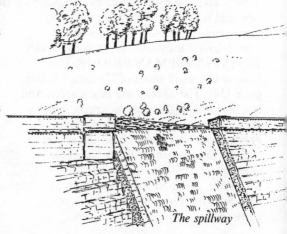

The spillway

the shoreline, and in a few minutes some of the drowned hut circles will appear. It is easier to appreciate the size of the stones used in their construction here than on the open moor where they are often "drowned" in Heather or Bracken.

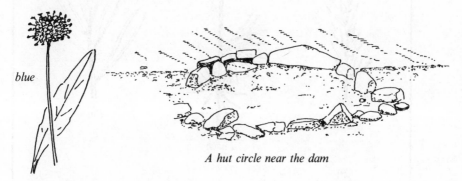

blue

Devil's-bit Scabious

A hut circle near the dam

white

Sneezewort

A hut circle near the fishermen's hut

If the water is high then from the dam take the upper path. Near the board walk, between it and the shore, is a clump of Sneezewort. This is the only time it has been noticed on these strolls. Another plant here, frequent in late summer, is Devil's-bit Scabious, so called because the Devil is said to have bitten off most of its root in a fit of temper.

****If you do not have a great deal of time then here is a suggestion for a shorter walk, suitable for any time of the year.

From the picnic area turn right and take the path to the dam. Cross the bridge just below it and walk along the shore of the reservoir as far as the kistvaen (See page 128). From that direction the small Rowan, behind which it lies, will be about a hundred yards past the lifebuoy to be seen across the water.

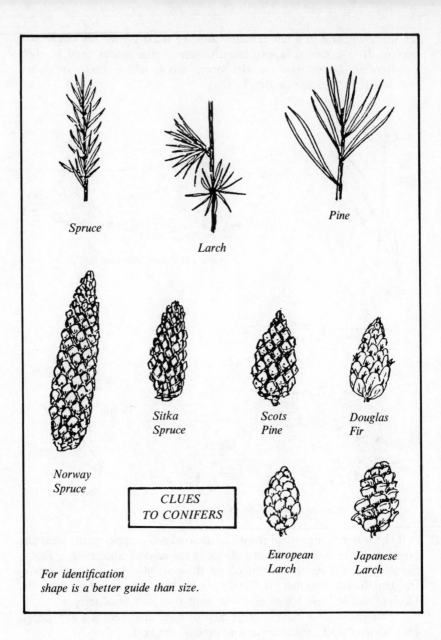

Spruce

Larch

Pine

Sitka
Spruce

Scots
Pine

Douglas
Fir

Norway
Spruce

CLUES
TO CONIFERS

European
Larch

Japanese
Larch

*For identification
shape is a better guide than size.*

CHRISTOPHER BOBBIN ON THE MOOR

There are prehistoric circles, and mighty stones in rows,
And logan stones that wobble with every wind that blows.
There are heaps of hills and tors and rivers to explore,
   But I read a book in a kistvaen when I go out on the moor.

There are wipses and wupses and wopses, and 'normous bugs with
    wings,
And masses of flies and skeeters, and hordes of buzzy things.
You can 'scape them all if you stand in the breeze on a windy tor.
   But I have a rest in a kistvaen when I go out on the moor.

There are woolly bears a-prowling, and dragons that can fly,
And tiger moths and el'phant hawks zooming through the sky;
And down in Tavy Cleave you can hear the brimstones roar.
   But I have a nap in a kistvaen when I go out on the moor.

Stroll round Widecombe-in-the-Moor

A village walkabout

Car Park: free car park in the village.

Grid Reference: 719768

Items of Interest: Old houses, a spacious church, a Saxon well, two inns, a Medieval firing range, wayside flowers.

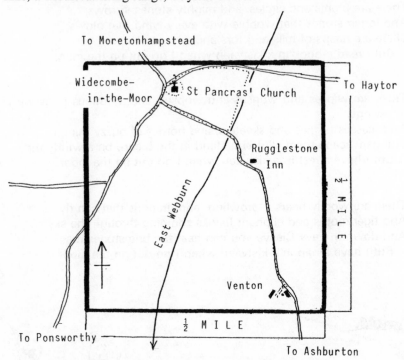

This really is an incredible village. That a small community in a deep valley in the middle of Dartmoor, only approachable by narrow lanes, should attract such hordes of visitors would be beyond belief to anyone who had not been there on a fine summer day. For Widecombe is on the coach operators' agenda. In spite of the difficult approach, and the little interest that the rest of the Moor (except Princetown?) has for many of those aboard, the coaches line up to disgorge parties from Art Societies, Garden Clubs, Women's Institutes, foreign students, Darbies and Joans, . . . you name it . . . and yet in spite of all this I still find Widecombe a pleasant place. It has a character all its own; its houses are built of the right materials, and (ignoring windows widened to display tourist souvenirs) they do have an unchanging centuries-old look.

Both of these signs
are worth investigating

The village is so small and compact that directions to explore it are inappropriate. But when you have exhausted the village itself—or the crowds have exhausted you—I'll suggest a half hour stroll that will take you out along a quiet lane and bring you back through a meadow.

At least five different guide books to Widecombe can be bought in the local shops, another five that contain just a chapter about the village, and two more devoted solely to Uncle Tom Cobley and his friends. So I'll be brief with background information and leave room to note several items that the other guides omit. For example, when I walked the suggested route of this stroll in late May the walls and hedgerows were massed with wild flowers. On the way round I listed 106 different species. Of course not all were yet in bloom. There would certainly be many more to be added on another visit later in the year. A few are illustrated on the next page to help with identification.

So leave the carpark and cross the road to examine what is probably the most photographed object in the valley—the village sign. On a typical day happy visitors queue up to photograph each other standing in front of it. Those of us who prefer the lonely horizons of the inner moor may find this abhorrent, but it is all part of Dartmoor!

Wander along the churchyard wall, noting the flowers and ferns that grow on and beyond it, and under a Sycamore a former entrance that has been walled up. There are some magnificent trees too on the Green, notably Horse Chestnut, Copper Beech and Sycamore. These are three species that would certainly not have been present when the villagers' medieval forbears used to practise archery here on a Sunday afternoon. In those days they practised not for fun but because the king said they had to.

133

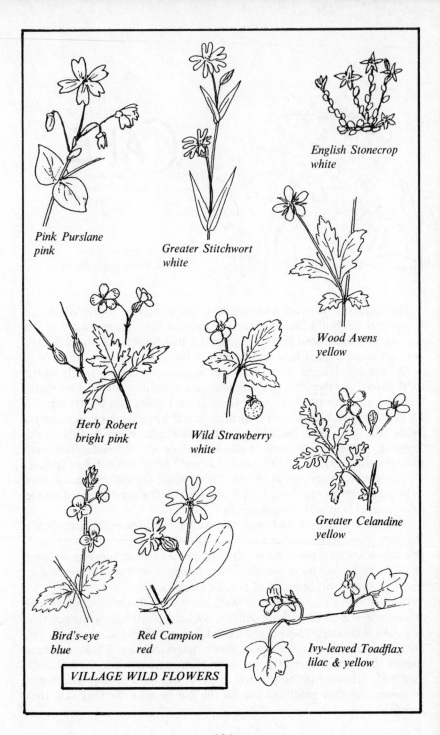

Pink Purslane
pink

Greater Stitchwort
white

English Stonecrop
white

Wood Avens
yellow

Herb Robert
bright pink

Wild Strawberry
white

Greater Celandine
yellow

Bird's-eye
blue

Red Campion
red

Ivy-leaved Toadflax
lilac & yellow

VILLAGE WILD FLOWERS

In a moment you round the end of Sexton Cottage, and find yourself in the throbbing heart of this miniature moorland metropolis. Stand awhile in rapture, or sit on the pedestal under the 120 year old Yew. From there you can see almost all there is of Widecombe village, though none of the wide combe in which it lies. It is clearly a friendly place. You can of course ignore the "Greetins vrum dere ol' Deb'n" and the request to "Cum in—tiz viddy yer", and stand aloof: but it would be much more fun to visit all the buildings you can, and the well stocked shops too.

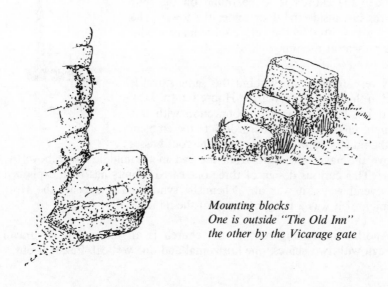

Mounting blocks
One is outside "The Old Inn"
the other by the Vicarage gate

The long Church House which fills one side of the square probably dates from the early 1500's. In its time it has been ale house, alms house, poor house, and school house. Under the veranda, whose monolithic columns are very similar to those in the church, stands a huge shell. This incongruous object was intended to be fired from a 15″ naval gun of the first world war.

Explore the churchyard: for those who want a rural view for their last rest this one would be hard to beat. The tall cross near the south door (See next page) is the original village cross. It once stood on one of the plinths in the square. If you are interested in epitaphs a pleasant ten minutes awaits you. The oldest stones have been used to shore up a cutting into the newer part of the cemetery. 1730 is the earliest date I could make out, though there are some earlier stones inside the church. The grave of local authoress Beatrice Chase is easily spotted. Look at its other face to read her real name.

The most terrifying event in all the history of Widecombe took place on the afternoon of Sunday 21st October, 1638, during a severe thunderstorm. The church, where a service was being held, was struck by lightning, and one of the tower pinnacles crashed through the roof. Four of the congregation were killed and many injured. The grave-stone of one of the victims and his wife can be seen near the chancel step. A horrifying account of the effects of the fireball that ran through the church is to be found on the four boards just inside the door under the tower. The story was written by the village schoolmaster who was present at the time.

A very different story about this same storm is told in the stroll from Warren House Inn (p. 115). That inn has also another connection with this church, in that its signboard depicts the emblem of the tinners' rabbits. Look up to the roof bosses

Village cross

above the nave—the third from the end in the middle row, above the altar. This curious design of three one-eared rabbits has been explained in several ways: it was an alchemists' symbol, it represents the Holy Trinity, or it was a favourite food of the miners.

Another interesting relic in the church is an unusual horse-drawn plough with two shares, one horizontal and one vertical. Puzzle it out.

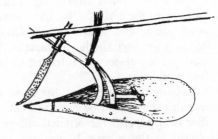

Part of a plough in the church

Tinners' rabbits

136

Back in the village walk down past the Post Office to the well. We are told it has been there for over a thousand years. A pity it is walled, roofed and boarded in. The pink flower with five petals but only two sepals, beside the streamlet close by, is Pink Purslane. You'll have seen lots of it round the village, but it has been here for less than fifty years, having come originally from North America.

Village well

"THE OLD INN"—part of which is 500 years old—may attract you for refreshment. It may be crowded, but where else can you have a meal seated at a Singer sewing machine table? The food and service are good, though few of the customers will speak with a Devon accent. However if you want the "real thing" a five-minute walk will take you to one of Dartmoor's smallest, quietest, and most unspoilt inns. Take the lane that skirts the churchyard on the south side, past "Glebe House". In less than a minute you will be among fields and meadows. The lane crosses the

Rugglestone Inn

The Old Inn

137

East Webburn and very soon a granite built house comes into view on the left. This is Rugglestone Inn, as unpretentious as The Old Inn is tourist-oriented. The accents in here are likely to be local ones, except perhaps for a few knowledgeable moor walkers who treasure its atmosphere and its good beer.

Five minutes further on along the lane is the picturesque hamlet of Venton. Higher Venton Farm has the date 1739 over its door, and decorations of plaited straw above the windows.

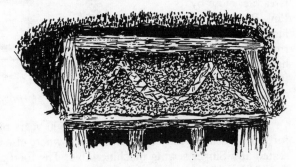

*Design of plaited straw
above a window
at Venton Farm*

The near end of the building was once the home of writer Beatrice Chase. Her private chapel is on the corner. Walk past it to make the acquaintance of Anthony, Gabriel and Michael.

Even the letterbox at the roadside is in keeping, being embossed with Queen's name and title—V.R.

Retrace your steps along the lane, but at the bridge across the East Webburn take the path to the right that runs through the meadow. This will bring you out after a short streamside stroll over a stile on to a road. Turn left into the village.

*"The Cathedral of the Moor"
seen from the meadow*

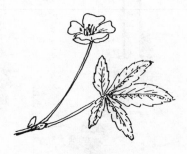

*Cinquefoil
yellow*

138

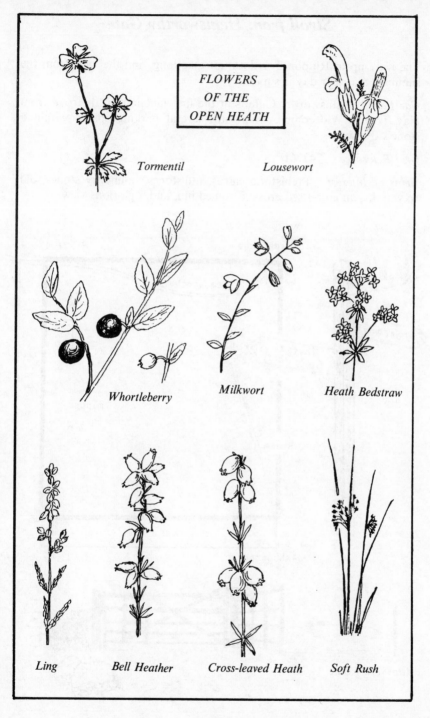

FLOWERS
OF THE
OPEN HEATH

Tormentil

Lousewort

Whortleberry

Milkwort

Heath Bedstraw

Ling

Bell Heather

Cross-leaved Heath

Soft Rush

Stroll from Hemsworthy Gate

The walk up to Rippon Tor does not take long, and the view from the summit on a clear day is superb.

Car Park: Hemsworthy Gate is at the first junction on the road from Hay Tor to Widecombe. There are several parking spaces within a stone's throw.

Grid Reference: 742761

Items of Interest: Prehistoric cairns, millstones, boundary stones, old waymarks, an embossed cross, a ruined inn, and a glorious view.

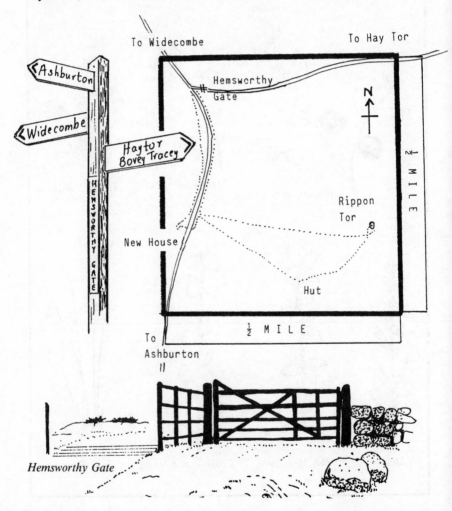

Hemsworthy Gate

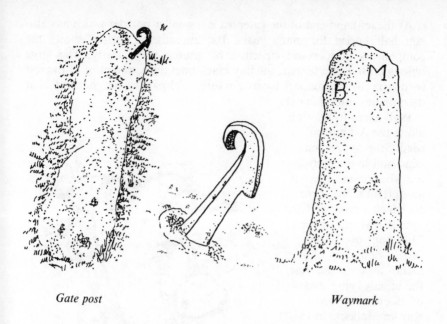

Gate post   _Waymark_

The modern signpost gives clear directions, but just opposite on the road-side bank is another waymark that has been there for possibly 150 years, and whose letters are still legible, if perhaps more enigmatic. B, M and A face the directions of Bovey Tracey, Manaton and Ashburton. Another indication of the former importance of this junction is the presence of the original gateposts. One still lies on the grassy verge with a fine iron hook projecting from it. The other has quite recently been built into the wall near the cattle grid. The bolt at the left hand end goes right through the stone. Its retaining nut is still in place.

Gate post

141

At the lefthand end of the gatepost is a smaller boulder which has also lain half buried for many years. Its unweathered surface shows the components and crystal structure of granite very clearly. The large oblong crystals are felspar, the tiny black ones mica, and most of the rest is quartz or a quartz/felspar mixture. Felspar is the mineral that decomposes into china clay.

Walk close to the wall along the Ashburton road. Stop at the first bend and look carefully into the corner. There is an upright stone there on which a cross and the initials RM can be seen. This stone marks the former boundary of a manor away to the west, the initials being those of its one time lord— Rawlin Mallock, in the 18th century. The stone is called Stittleford's Cross, but the origin of this name remains a mystery.

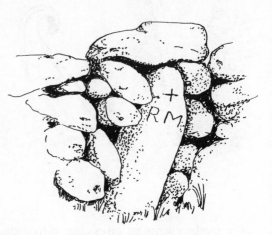

Stittleford's Cross

Continue along the road for a few hundred yards, wondering now and again how the "grounders"—the huge boulders at the base of the wall—were levered into position. On the hillside to the right a pattern of lines can be made out: these are the ruinous walls of 19th century fields superimposed on a small Bronze Age settlement.

When you reach this hunting gate go through, fasten it securely, and take the easiest route up the slope to Rippon Tor.

On the next page are illustrated some flowers to look for on the way. The yellow Tormentil is one of Dartmoor's most widespread flowers. Lousewort which is purplish

Rippon Tor

142

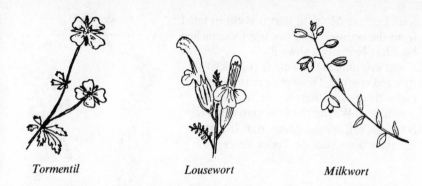

Tormentil   Lousewort   Milkwort

grows in damp places. The delicate Milkwort has flowers of three colours, blue, pink, or white. Blue ones are the commonest. It owes its name to its former use, as a sort of tea, by nursing mothers.

On the highest point of the tor is a triangulation pillar. The stones of the prehistoric cairn had to be cleared aside until solid rock could be found on which to erect it. Here you are 1,560 feet above sea level, having climbed up 250 feet from the road. Take time to stand and admire the view. There are two more cairns, perhaps concealing burial chambers, along the ridge to the southeast. I often wonder whether, if there really are bodies of local chieftains beneath these heaps, their owners chose their burial site before they died. In the rock beside the pillar is a shallow rock basin which has some large felspar crystals showing. (For information about rock basins see page 66.)

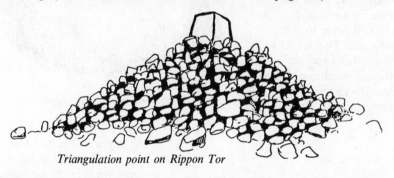

Triangulation point on Rippon Tor

Just below the cairn are the remains of what was once perhaps a shepherd's hut. Far beyond lies the estuary of the River Teign and the Channel. Turn round slowly in a full circle. If the air is really clear some of Dartmoor's finest tors and remotest hills will be in view, and far to the north and northeast the lines of Exmoor and the Brendons in Somerset mark the horizon.

From the summit go down about 40 yards towards Hemsworthy Gate. There, half buried, lies a crude cross. This is unlike all the others to be

143

found on the Moor in that it is cut in relief from the bedrock, and not from a detached boulder. Nobody knows if it was ever intended to cut it completely free and erect it. There appear to be as many theories as there are authorities on the subject. Waymark? Christian symbol? Scarer of evil spirits? Memorial? It almost certainly dates back to Tudor times.

Rippon Tor cross

Millstone ...

Now turn half left and walk downhill in the direction of a patch of green turf by the road, where there are a few trees. In a moment or two you will come to this millstone. This seems to be another example (though much more recent than the cross) of an uncompleted task. Did the

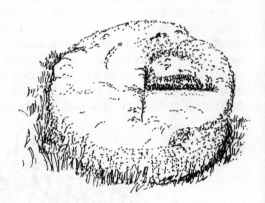

... or perhaps a cheese press?

top surface offer too much difficulty? Or did the stonemason give up for some other reason?

Turn half left again and go uphill (southwards). Follow a low stony bank—an ancient reave—which runs to the right of the summit. After a short distance another abandoned millstone is to be

Millstone

144

seen, leaning out from the bank. A much thinner one this, and still only roughly shaped.

If you have time to dally on the heights there is yet another millstone to be found, or the other two cairns to be explored.

Now head southwest down the gentle slope towards the rocks beyond the wall. About half way to the wall bear half right to the scanty ruins

Stonecutter's hut

of a small hut. It is said to have been a stonecutter's shelter. I wonder if the frustrated mason whose work still lies on the hilltop sheltered here.

Go out on to the road through the gate and turn left. At the corner of the wall this stone lies on the bank. 'A' stands for Ashburton. The parish boundary comes right up to here.

A hundred yards further on are the obvious remains of some small enclosures, and an area of smooth turf. Here once stood New

Parish boundary stone

House, a wayside inn. This spot is just under half way from Ashburton to Chagford on the most practicable cross-moorland route. Both towns were important centres of the tin and the woollen industries, while from the south lime was also carried this way to many moorland farms, so for a good many centuries a considerable amount of traffic passed here: the inn would have provided a welcome break. The last landlord was named Foales, and it was his field walls on the slopes of Pil Tor that were noted

New House Inn

earlier on the walk. They are known as Foales' Arrishes (fieldlets). The Hawthorns now leaning along the inn walls make striking silhouettes against a winter sky in the late afternoon.

Walk back along the road now, and after a little while use the faint track that runs parallel to it on the left. Head towards the signpost. On your left is a line of six stones marking a parish boundary. The first two are in very marshy ground, but you can made for the one that at first looks triangular, and follow the line back to the road junction. The sixth stone is quite small, and the one after that is Stittleford's Cross in the wall.

On this side is the parish of Widecombe in the Moor

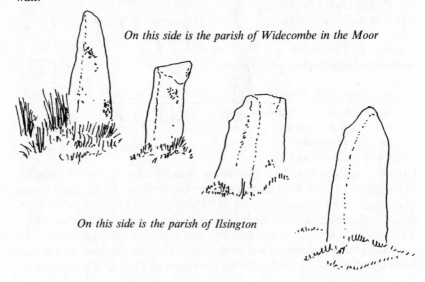

On this side is the parish of Ilsington

146

Stroll on Haytor Down

Easy going with no wet places

Car Park: at the lowest of the car parks at Haytor Rocks (the one with the toilets) on the Bovey Tracey–Widecombe road.

Grid Reference: 765772

Items of Interest: Britain's hardest granite, Devon's first railway, a pond in a quarry, an apple crusher.

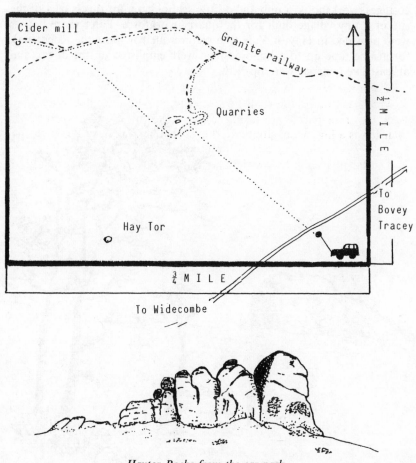

Haytor Rocks from the car park

From the car park walk up the grassy track towards the pair of trees in front of the flat-topped mound that is to the right of the tor. These mounds are the waste heaps from a large quarry just behind them. The various quarries on Haytor Down used to supply the hardest granite available in Britain, and were worked, somewhat spasmodically, for about fifty years during the last century. Among the better known buildings incorporating Haytor granite are the British Museum and the western face of London Bridge. (The eastern face was built of a deeper coloured stone from near Princetown.) This is the bridge that was demolished and rebuilt in Arizona. I wonder which way it faces now.

The trees you are heading for turn out to be Larches—a wind battered photogenic pair in a romantic setting. Nearby is a third more stunted one, an old gatepost, ruined walls, depressions and rubbly mounds of unguessed origin. Romantic? Yes, a hundred years ago there were cottages, workshops, a pub and a little school here, for this is part of the site of a tiny village built for the quarry workforce. Later more houses were provided in Haytor Vale (the picturesque row near the Rock Inn), for at one time up to a hundred men were employed on the down, and at least five quarries were opened.

Tors, Larches, and a vanished village

Haytor village—perhaps it looked something like this

Climb up the large heather covered mound. Below is a cutting which was the entrance to a small quarry. Turn left along the fence as far as the gate. Go through and down into the large quarry. Here is a little world, sheltered, colourful, and remote from the madding crowd. Apart from a

*The largest
of the Haytor quarries*

few short-lived activities—for instance the cutting of granite for Exeter War Memorial in 1919—this hole in the earth's surface has been left in the care of Time and Nature for over a century. A pool has formed, and animals and plants have moved in. Man has provided a helping hand now and again: the goldfish in the deeper pool could hardly have found their way there unaided, though I couldn't see any the last time I searched. There was however a patch of White Water-lily, and more surprisingly, a few flowers of the Fringed Water-lily. This is smaller than the common yellow one: it has fringed petals and only 5 stamens. Perhaps water birds brought in the seeds.

Another uncommon plant here, which never seems to be illustrated in books, is

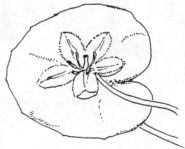

Fringed Water-lily

150

an orange fungus that grows on dead leaves that have been lying for a long time in shallow water. Its botanical name could be translated as Little Marsh Hat. Then in season there are dragonflies, whirligigs, and a host of other insects.

Little Marsh Hat

There are also a number of relics of the industry that once went on. Just below you are these two, probably last used about 1920.

Winch

Part of a derrick

Here are some more relics for your "collection".

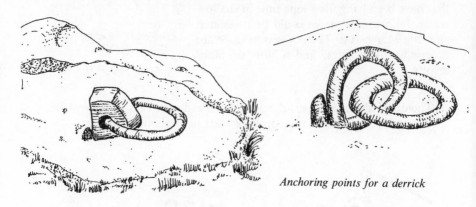

Anchoring points for a derrick

With imagination the quarry can be peopled with fifty workers digging, drilling, blasting, hammering, heaving, using winches and derricks, loading blocks of stone on to trolleys, assembling horse teams, measuring, surveying .... Dress the workmen in stout clothes of the 1850's, remove the water from the quarry floor, add a cacophony of shouts, rumbles, and iron striking stone, and there you have it—a sound film in glorious technicolour!

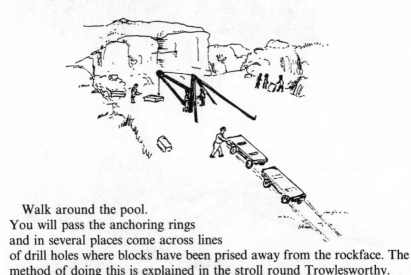

Walk around the pool.
You will pass the anchoring rings
and in several places come across lines
of drill holes where blocks have been prised away from the rockface. The method of doing this is explained in the stroll round Trowlesworthy.

After exploring the workings you can either return the same way to the gate or continue round the pool nearly to the vertical face that drops into the water, and there climb the short steep path. This will take you on round above the smaller quarry to rejoin the path up to the gate.

Once outside the fence turn left down the side of the cutting and at the end bear left along a track. Almost immediately you will be walking along the oldest railway in Devon, opened in September 1820. The problem of transporting the granite for shipment to London was solved by building this line from the Haytor Quarries to the already existing canal at Teigngrace about seven and a half miles away. There the stone was loaded into barges and carried to Teignmouth for onward passage by sea.

The rails were made from the best local material available, granite—a granite moreover specially renowned for its resistance to friction.

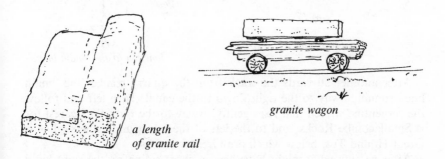

granite wagon

*a length
of granite rail*

The rail blocks were mostly from 2 to 5 feet long, the shorter ones being on the curves. The wagon wheels had no flanges: they simply ran along the outer edges of the rails which were fashioned into an L-shaped cross-section. The first few rails on the right show clearly how little wear has been caused by the transport of thousands of tons of stone. Before long you come to a place where a branch line comes in from the left, and then the track crosses some old mining gulleys. Just beyond these a siding goes off to the right.

Here and at other junctions it is interesting to examine the way in which the rails have been cut. When at the "Points" it is not possible to move the rails then another system has to be used to direct the trucks along the required track. It is thought that a wedge-shaped toggle, like the one illustrated, may have been used. At some of the junctions the hole into which the toggle was inserted can be seen, but curiously this is not always so.

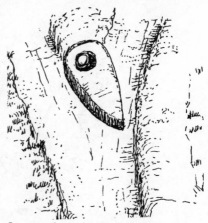

Iron toggle at the "points"

153

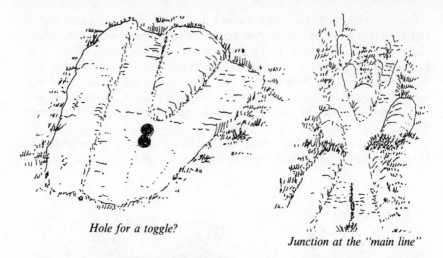

Hole for a toggle?

Junction at the "main line"

After another 50 yards the track from the quarry reaches the "main line" running away to the right down to the canal. Turn left and follow the serpentine stretch that rises gently. Away to the right the nearest tor is Smallacombe Rocks, and to the left of these just under the skyline is Great Hound Tor, below which are Greator Rocks.

After passing what might have been a short siding on the right hand side you come to a fork. The straight-ahead branch goes to several small quarries and the right hand one runs down to the large quarry at the end of the line, under Holwell Tor. Take the right fork. Notice that now you are walking downhill. This is the only stretch along the whole way where laden wagons had to be pulled uphill. It is said that up to nineteen horses were needed here to haul a train of perhaps a dozen wagons loaded with maybe 30 tons of granite. It is probable that along the remainder of the

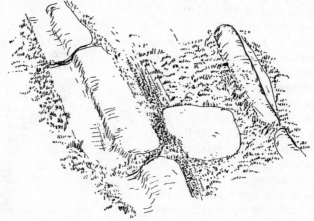

Rails of granite

154

journey to Teigngrace the well engineered downhill gradient would have allowed the horses to be unhitched. Some would walk down ready to haul the empty wagons back up again. The "engine driver" preferred to trust his brakes rather than run the risk of laden trucks overtaking his "horse power".

Two minutes beyond the junction will bring you to this stone just beside the track. It is thought to have been intended as the base of a small cider mill. A vertical stone would have rolled round inside the flange to crush the apples. It was probably abandoned when a hammer blow in the wrong place damaged it irreparably.

Part of a broken cider mill

This is the furthest point of the stroll. Pause to admire the outline of Great Hound Tor, now on the skyline, and then turn back.

This time when you reach the last junction take the grassy path which leads up the slope through the heather. It soon joins another one going towards the big quarry.

Great Hound Tor

155

This is a good area in which to taste the whortleberries when they are in season—July or August. If you come from beyond Devon you may perhaps call them Bilberries, but here they are simply "worts". Two of the three common species of heather are also plentiful on this slope, Ling and Bell Heather.

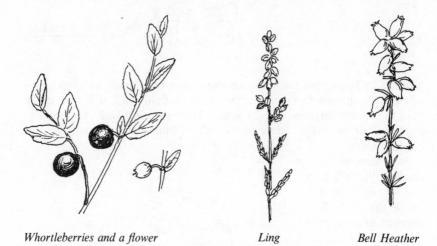

Whortleberries and a flower   *Ling*   *Bell Heather*

As the foot of the waste heaps climb up to the fence, turn right and follow it round above the quarry. In a few minutes the car park will be in sight, and beyond it, if the weather favours you, the sea at Teignmouth.

Hay Tor itself is not far away, and would make a grand diversion before returning to the road . . . while down in the car park there will almost certainly be an ice cream van.

By way of postscript:

It is not often recorded that the two enormous masses at Haytor Rocks have separate names. The rock mass farthest from the road is named Low Man while the other one, or the two together, have accumulated all these names over the years:

Haytor Rocks	Hay Tor
Hey Tor	High Tor
Hea Tor	Idetor
Aether Rocks	Ather Tor
Arter Rocks	

I F F

If only Kipling could read this!

If you can plod for miles through mists unbroken
   To rest content upon an unnamed tor,
Or walk for sunlit hours with no word spoken
   Except a skylark singing o'er the moor;

If you can keep your feet and not go sliding
   Off stones that glisten in a laughing stream,
Or through a quaking bog go boldly striding
   To pick your route with confidence supreme;

If you can leap from hag to hag so lightly
   You never soil your jeans with soggy peat;
If you can run and jump and judge it rightly
   And never land with one foot in a leat;

If you have learned the course of Teign and Okement
   By trudging through the mire to where they start;
If you can understand just what the bloke meant
   'Oo zed 'e zee'd zum piskies up the Dart;

   If you abhor to hear the tourists shouting,
      Or watch them flying kites from Haytor Rocks:
   Then get your map and compass for an outing.
      Be off!—On Cut Hill there's a letterbox.

157

INDEX TO PLANT AND ANIMAL ILLUSTRATIONS

Some plants and birds appear more than once in these pages. They are only indexed more than once if the illustrations are different.